Olga Jevrić

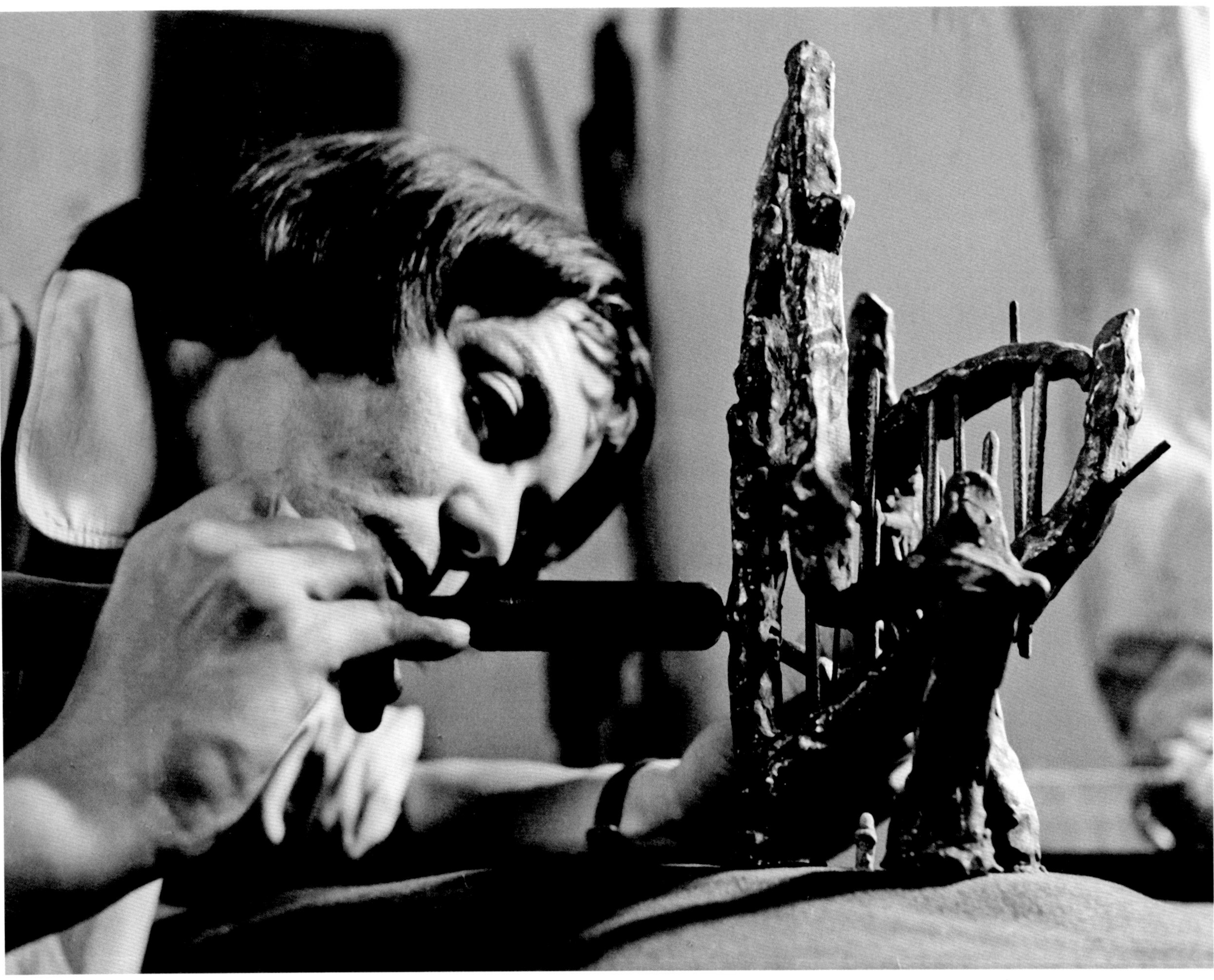

OLGA JEVRIĆ

PEER Ridinghouse

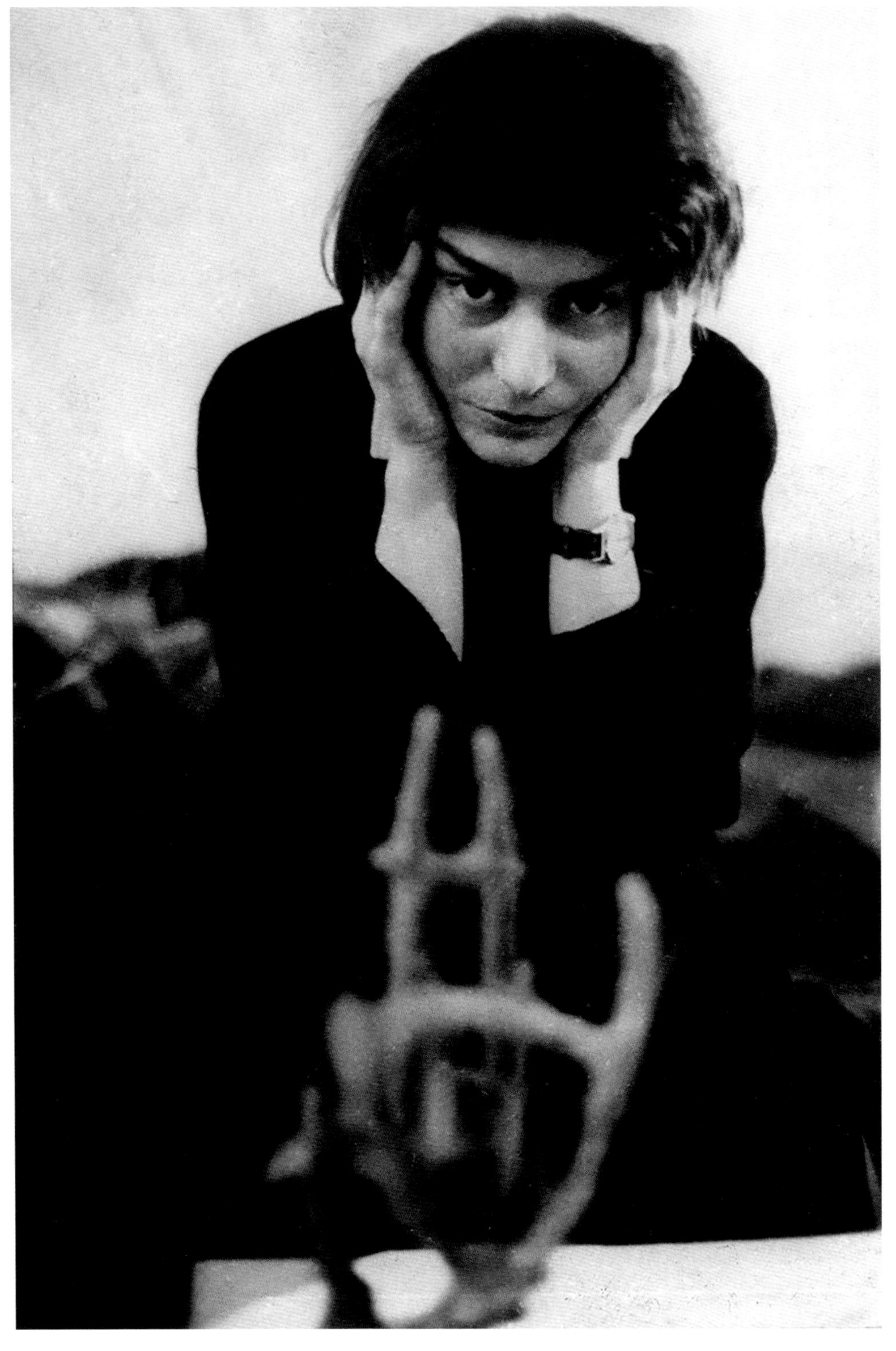

Contents

Preface

This publication celebrates the presentation of Olga Jevrić's work in London and is the first English-language examination of this remarkable artist.

I first encountered Olga Jevrić's work in 2016 at an exhibition of her *Proposals for Monuments* that was presented by the Henry Moore Institute in Leeds. Like many of the visitors to her exhibition at PEER three years later, my response had been immediate and visceral. The sculptures had a freshness, vitality and impact that belied both their date of production and their modest size. I also felt an inexplicable closeness to the work – their fluency as sculptural objects seemed to communicate in a direct and urgent way. This strange sense of familiarity was accompanied by a mild sense of embarrassment that I had not heard of the artist before.

A short while later, when visiting Fedja Klikovac at Handel Street Projects, I noticed that he had a book about Jevrić, an artist whom he had personally known since the 1980s in Belgrade and had greatly admired until her death in 2014. He told me how celebrated she was and still is in the former Yugoslavia, but also how her work was rarely on public display. When he explained that he had been planning to exhibit her work in London, and that he had been instrumental in securing the acquisition of nine works for Tate, I proposed he might like to co-curate an exhibition at PEER.

There are many individuals who have enabled this project. First and foremost I am thankful to Fedja Klikovac for sharing his knowledge of and passion for Jevrić's work and for the informative first-hand account of the cultural landscape in Belgrade in his introduction. Two of Britain's most distinguished artists, Richard Deacon and Phyllida Barlow, have been involved in the project from very early on, which is something that I believe Jevrić would have most heartily approved of. They contributed their ideas to the elegant exhibition design and have both written texts for this publication. Deacon's text tells his story of encountering Olga Jevrić's work at the Museum of Contemporary Art in Belgrade and then having the opportunity to meet the artist. Barlow's response is in the form of a prose-poem that both reflects upon Jevrić's work and explores her personal relationship to sculptural practice in Europe since her formative years as a student in the 1960s. The text by artist Joan Key came about as a response to Jevrić's '43 Theses' and is a more philosophical reading of the artist's work. Ješa Dengeri, one of Serbia's most esteemed art historians and a lifelong friend of Jevrić's, has written an illuminating essay exploring Jevrić's work and its context.

The three institutional lenders to the PEER exhibition have been enormously supportive throughout. I would especially like to thank Žaklina Marković, Curator, and Dušan Otaševic, Academician, at the Serbian Academy of Sciences and Arts, Belgrade; Dejan Vucetić, Curator, and Filip Brusić-Renaud, Director, at Heritage House, Belgrade; and Zoran Erić, Chief Curator, and Dr. Rajka Bošković, Advisor, at the Museum of Contemporary Art Belgrade.

The project was also made possible with the kind cooperation of Jevrić's family, and in particular Milesa Radivojević and Marko Djukić. We are very grateful to the Henry Moore Foundation for financial support and would also specifically like to thank Serbian Ambassador Aleksandra Joksimović and the Ministry for Culture of the Republic of Serbia. My most sincere thanks also go to Rosa Harvest at PEER for her incredible work on the exhibition production, to Robert Dalrymple for his beautiful book design, and to Sophie Kullmann of Ridinghouse for coordinating the publication.

Finally, I would like to thank Karsten Schubert for agreeing to publish this book in partnership with PEER. Although it turned out to be the last book that he was to commission, like so many newcomers to Jevrić's work, Karsten's enthusiasm was instantaneous.

Ingrid Swenson
Director, PEER

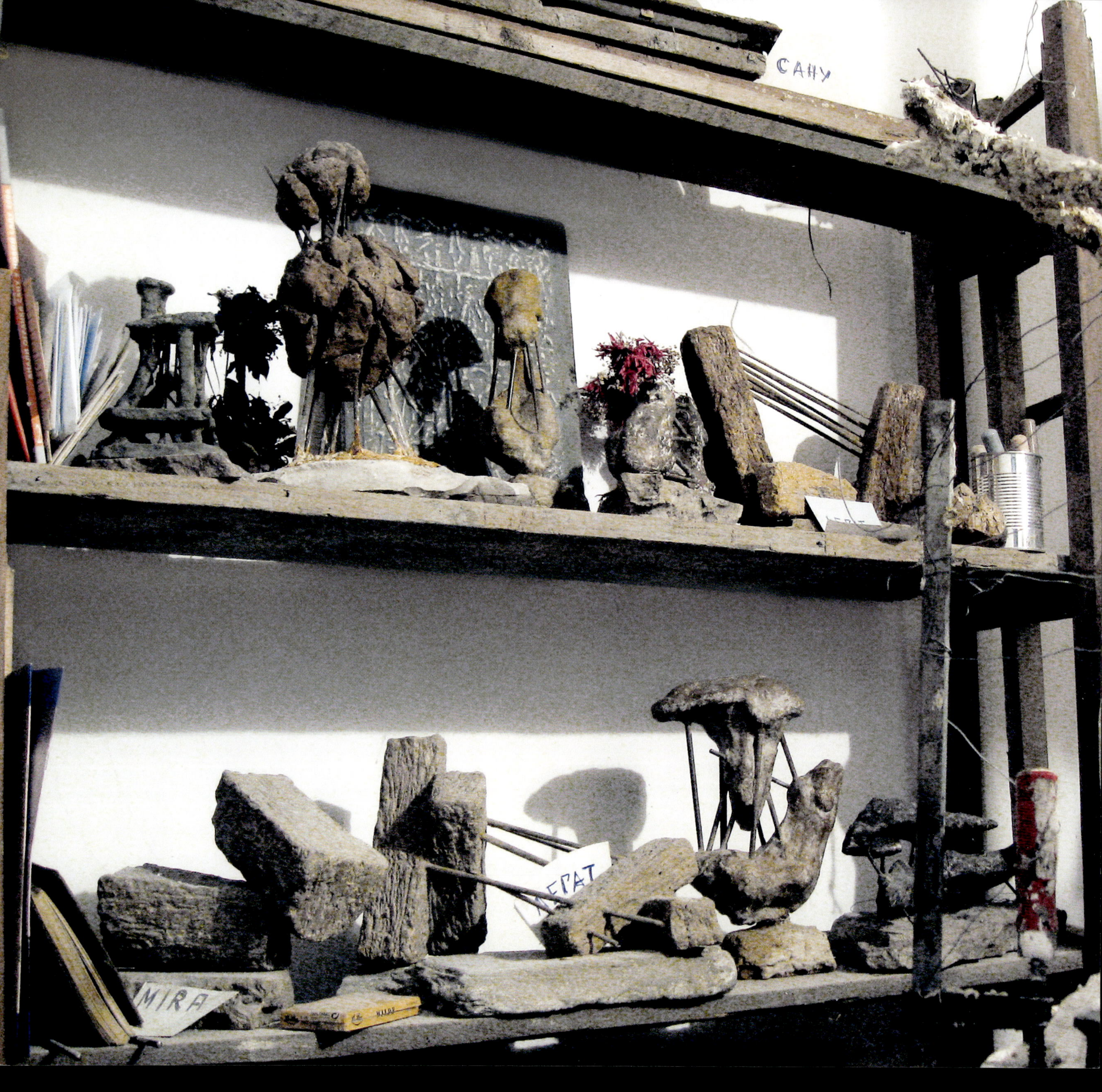
САНУ
KEPAT
MIRA

Olga Jevrić:
Spatial Compositions

Fedja Klikovac

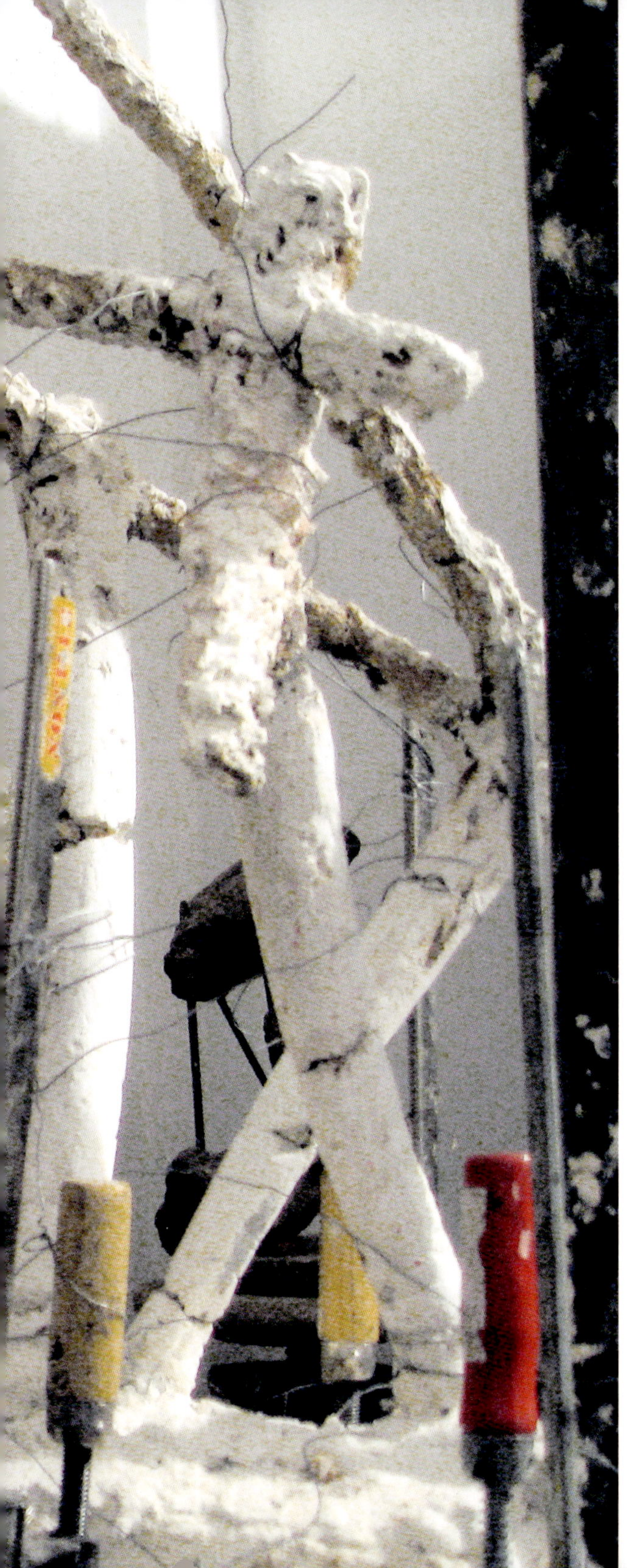

My first encounter with Olga Jevrić's work was
in 1981 at the wonderful solo exhibition at the
Museum of Contemporary Art in Belgrade.[1]
Comprising 141 sculptures, it was the most
comprehensive survey of her work to date. The
second time I saw it was in 1988 at the gallery
of the Student Cultural Centre (SKC Gallery).[2]
This too was an important exhibition, placing her
work in the contemporary context – a time when
younger artists were looking to the past and
re-examining modernism.[3] It also held a special
importance for those of us working in and around
the gallery, resurrecting as it did an interest
in a new kind of sculpture. Both of these were
inspirational shows, and they had a significant
impact on the art scene of the time.

   The work of Olga Jevrić has a special place in
the pantheon of postwar European sculpture.
The two exhibitions of Jevrić's work at PEER
and Handel Street Projects present works from
all phases of her long career, illustrating how
her interest in pure form and structure turned
increasingly in the direction of a poetics of space.
Her first solo exhibition in Belgrade, *Spatial*

Olga Jevrić's studio,
Belgrade, 17 April 2009

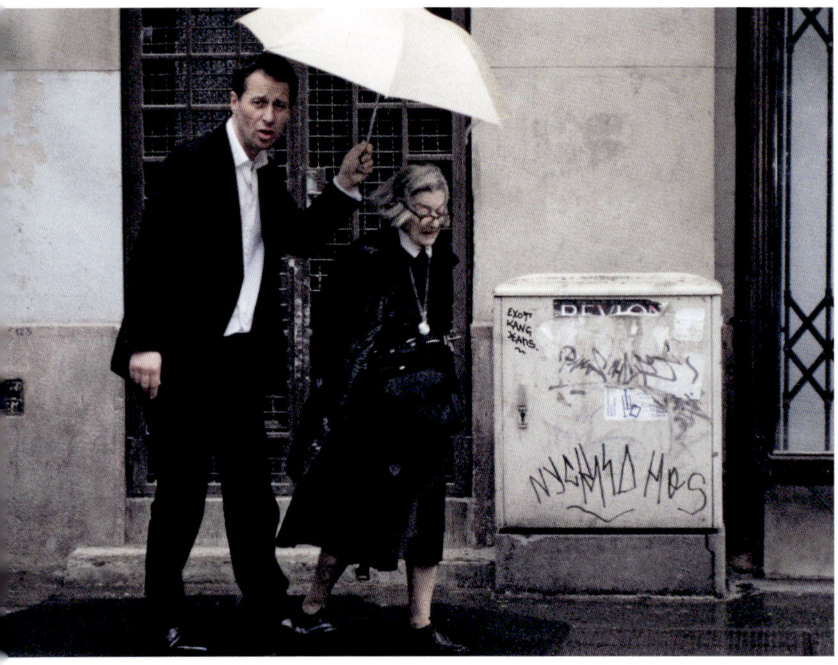

Compositions, took place in 1957, eight years after she graduated, confirming her position as a 'serious artist'. Subsequently, she was asked to contribute to the Yugoslav pavilion at the 29th Venice Biennale in 1958, where she exhibited eight works alongside four other Yugoslav artists, drawing acclaim from a number of prominent artists and critics.[4]

The Venice presentation was followed by an exhibition at Galleria Notizie in Turin in 1959,[5] and in 1961 her work was shown in Britain for the first time in a three-person exhibition at Drian Galleries.[6] That same year she took part in a group exhibition at the Tate Gallery, *Contemporary Yugoslav Painting and Sculpture*, and in 1970 was included in *Contemporary Yugoslav Sculpture*

at the Hayward Gallery. More recently, in 2016, a selection of eleven small works were shown as *Olga Jevrić: Proposals for Monuments* at the Henry Moore Institute in Leeds.

Born in Belgrade in 1922, Jevrić developed her unique visual language at a time when, amid the ideological constraints of Socialist realism, there was little space for personal expression. Yugoslavia's 1948 schism with the Soviet Union marked the start of a new era for the country. During the 1950s and 1960s a number of reforms were introduced, which helped the young Yugoslav society position itself between East and West. Workers' Self-Management, a unique brand of socialism,[7] was introduced, and in 1956 the Non-Aligned Movement was founded on Brioni island (formalised in Belgrade in 1961). New cultural contacts were established, which resulted in a number of exhibitions travelling from Europe and the United States to various cities in Yugoslavia: *Contemporary French Art* in 1952; *Henry Moore* in 1955; *Modern Art in the United States: A Selection from the Collections of the Museum of Modern Art, New York* in 1956; and *Contemporary Italian Art* in 1956–57.[8] In 1958–59 the important architecture exhibition *Built in USA: Post-War Architecture*, originally mounted in 1953 at the Museum of Modern Art in New York, also toured Yugoslavia.[9]

Jevrić's first abstract works in the early 1950s consisted of a series of proposals for memorial monuments, none of which were realised in the monumental way she had envisaged. Principally this was because these sculptures – or 'spatial compositions', as she called them – belonged to the domain of 'high modernism',[10] being abstractions of a non-associative type. Jevrić

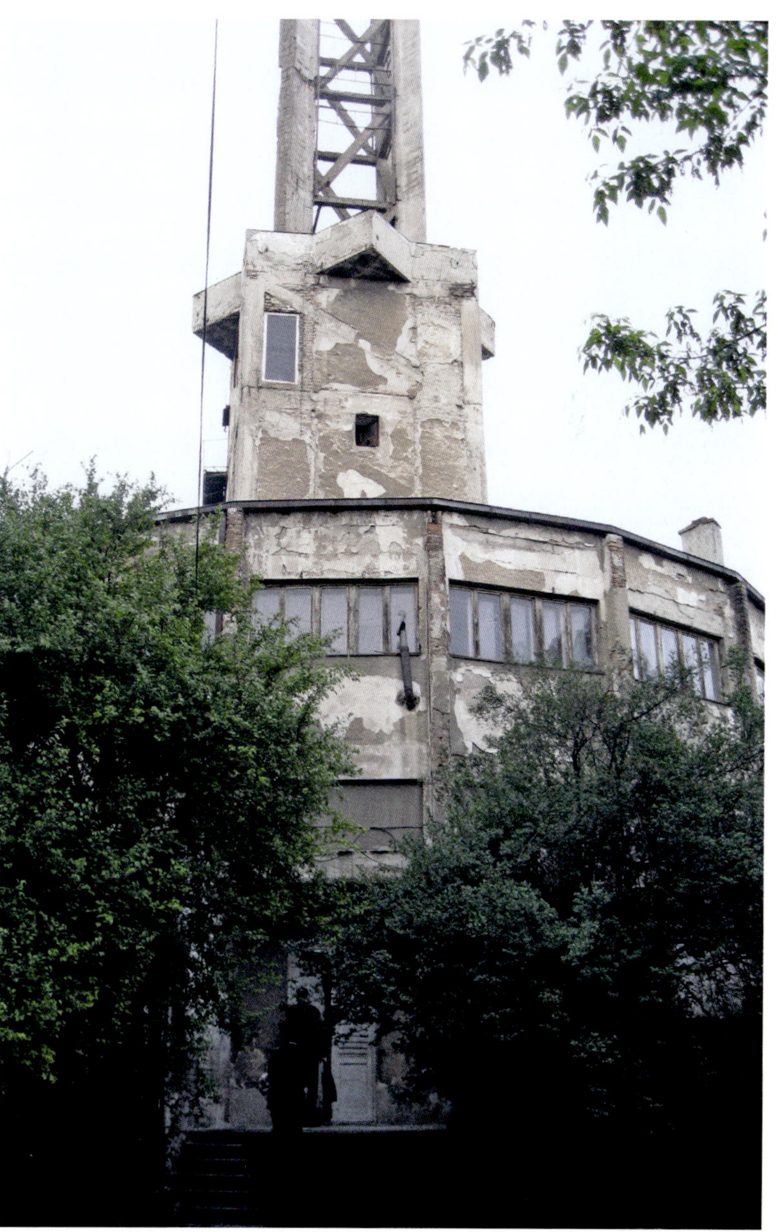

Former Central Pavilion (known as Kula, or 'Tower'), Staro sajmište, Belgrade, dated 1937. Jevrić's studio was situated on the ground floor

typified them both as a departure 'from learned schemes' and as an opportunity 'to be true to myself and to give myself freedom'.[11] Her early work is fundamentally linked to medieval stećci,[12] monolithic medieval tombstones that are found across Bosnia and Herzegovina, Serbia, Croatia and Montenegro, leading Jevrić to assert that she could not have made her sculptures anywhere other than in her own country. They are, she explained, informed by 'war, uncertainty, the slaughter of innocent people, social upheavals and disorder of all social norms'.[13]

Jevrić claimed that her sculptures derived from 'the system of constructing based on dialectical structural principles'. To understand phenomena, according to this view, demands that we treat them as a set of relations among elements. Jevrić's commentary on her own work suggests an interest in both structuralism and dialectical materialist philosophy; yet in spite of the pervasiveness of formalist tendencies in her work, her passion for materials is always clear. Although she made bronzes, her true material was concrete mixed with iron dust, which would oxidise to give her works their unique colour and texture. Jevrić's choice of concrete and iron in her work of the 1950s and 1960s – a period when other sculptors were also replacing traditional media with industrial materials – reflected a wider omnipresence of these materials in Yugoslavia. State-of-the-art modernist towns such as New Belgrade were being built at a rapid pace, and sculpture and architecture now seemed to share the same language.[14] If these materials were giving shape to a new Yugoslavia, then they were also prompting new ways of making sculpture. From now on, 'sculpting'

Details from Olga Jevrić's studio,
17 April 2009

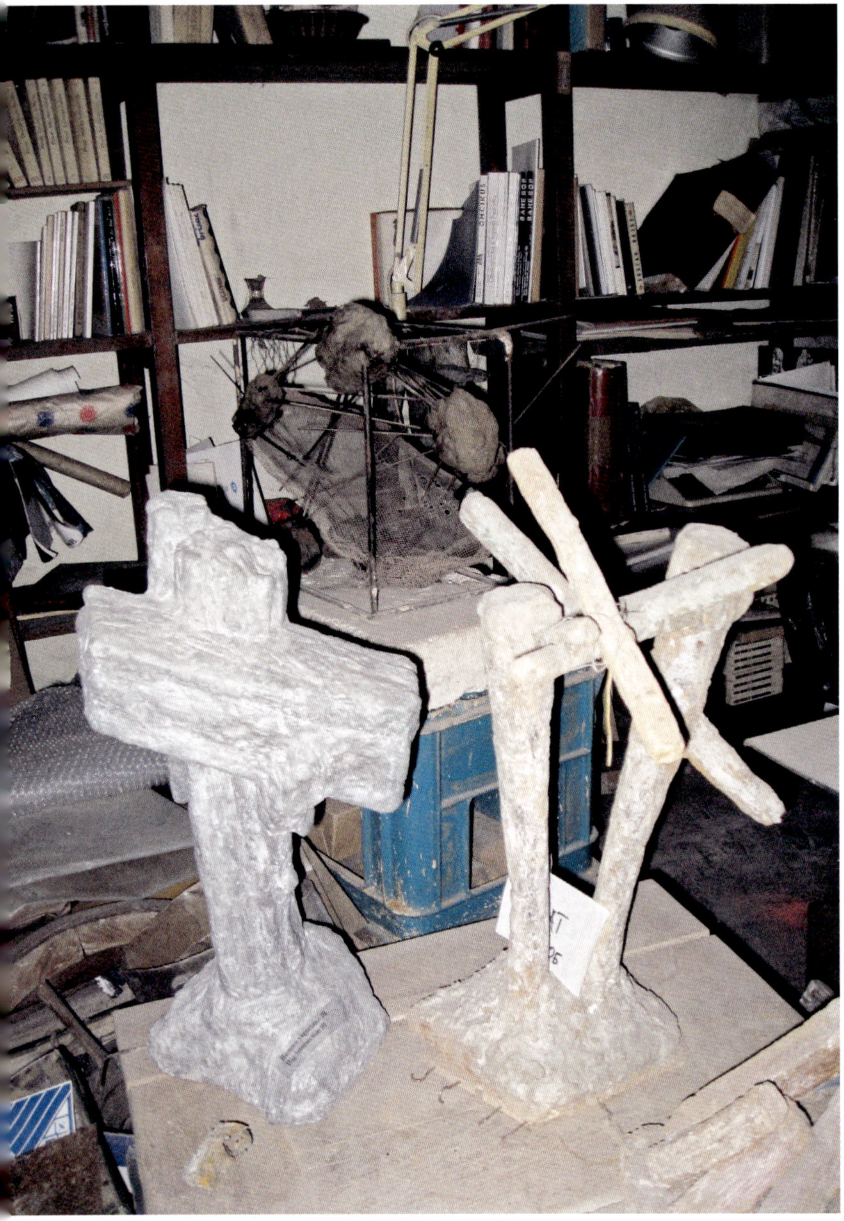

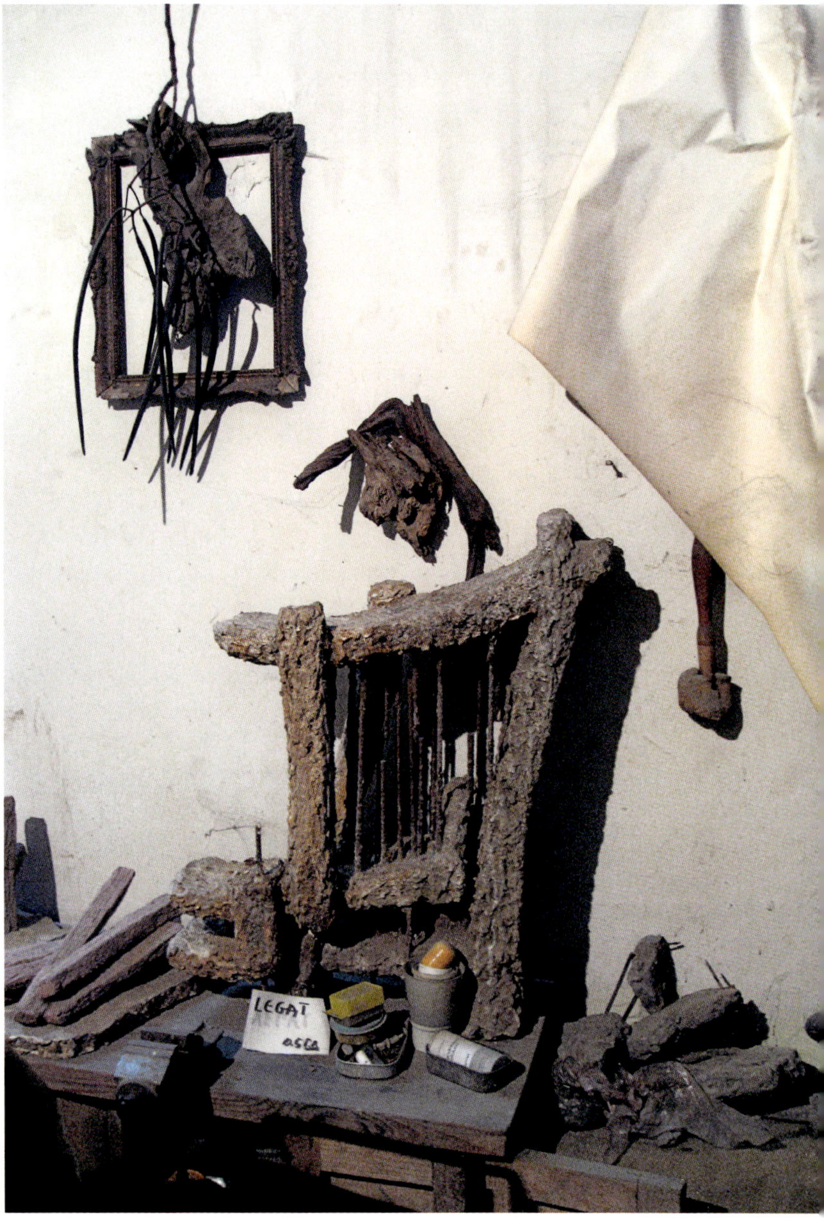

would often be referred to by Jervić and others as 'building'.

Over time Jervić deployed a variety of techniques. In her early works, the initial idea would find form in clay, which was then covered with molten metal, most often iron. Later, having arrived at her preferred combination of cement mixed with iron oxide – a compound she called 'ferroxide' – she would produce larger works in parts, constructing a frame of wooden slats which she would wrap with wire mesh and then cover with the ferroxide mixture, the elements held together by iron rods. These works represented a leap from a sculpture of the body, determined by finite closed volumes, to unbound, open spatial abstract sculpture. As a result of this shift they succeeded in uniting opposites, bringing together an expressive, rebellious, existentialist attitude with decidedly constructivist tendencies.

Small but significant changes can be identified in her subsequent work. The compact early objects gave way to more disjointed, skeletal pieces, while in the later works iron rods are buried deep in the fabric of the sculpture before disappearing altogether in her final works, becoming architectural if not minimalist in form but, once again, highly expressive.

Jevrić's work owed a lot to her early interest in music. She studied piano at university before enrolling at the Belgrade Academy of Fine Arts, but stopped playing because of painful cramps in her hands. Indeed, the shapes and formal aspects of the hammers and strings of a piano are ubiquitous in her work, materialised in nails, wires and lumps of matter connected with metal spines. She spoke of music as itself a spatial event, with melodic lines spreading through time and space, ascending and descending, with scales, pauses, intervals, silence and rhythm all contributing to the construction of her 'spatial compositions'.

Although music is so often seen as the most abstract art form, Jevrić's ambition was perhaps to give it concrete form. She was equally fascinated by the internal workings of the human body. A favourite place was the Natural History Museum in Belgrade (as well as other similar museums abroad), and she described her excitement at seeing for the first time human organs, lungs, hearts and livers, together with the organic phenomena of crystallisation and growth. It is perhaps in the coalescence of these two sets of interests – music and the body – that we find the vibrant, creative matrix of Jervić's work and its concern with how bodies interlink, connect, join and separate.

The last time I met Olga Jevrić was on 24 January 2014, at her studio in one of the massive former Belgrade Fair Buildings.[15] I visited her with Frances Morris, then the director of Tate's international collection. Smoking incessantly, Olga played Vivaldi on a small tape recorder as she recalled her early days as part of the extraordinary artistic community housed on that site, which was constructed in 1937 as an exhibition centre to host world trade events and expositions; its rich cultural history includes being the location of the first TV transmission in the Balkans, in 1938. Later, the Yugoslav premiere of Samuel Beckett's *Waiting for Godot* took place there, in 1954 in the studio of the artist Mića Popović, [16] and the art critics Gillo Dorfles, Jean Cassou and Herbert Read visited Jevrić in her studio in the former Central Pavilion (known as Kula, or 'Tower'). But the Fair complex also had a dark side – one reflected in the work of many of the artists who worked there from the 1950s onwards – as during the Second World War it was the site of the Sajmište concentration camp, where tens of thousands of people were detained and killed. Jevrić was one of the last artists to work there, retaining her studio until her death. During my visit, Jevrić also mentioned her trip to the United States in 1966, where she stayed for a year on a Ford Foundation Fellowship.[17] An exhibition with David Smith was proposed at the time, but she wasn't able to secure support for this on her return to Belgrade. Little did she know that their work would meet posthumously in London as part of the Tate collection.[18] Jevrić was to die shortly after our visit, on 10 February 2014.

NOTES

1 The exhibition was curated by Ješa Denegri. The Museum of Contemporary Art in Belgrade opened in 1965, designed by the architects Ivan Antić (1923–2005) and Ivanka Raspopović (1930–2015). It reopened in 2017 after a lengthy period of renovation and restoration.

2 The exhibition was curated by Biljana Tomić, who had been running programmes at the gallery for many years, bringing the European avant-garde to Belgrade as well as supporting young local and Yugoslav artists. The first generation of Yugoslav conceptual artists, including Marina Abramović, Era Milivojević, Zoran Popović, Neša Paripović and Raša Todosijević, gathered at SKC Gallery, producing and showing some iconic works.

3 Gianni Vattimo's book *The End of Modernity (La fine della modernità)*, published in 1985 and translated into Serbian in 1991, was highly influential around this time.

4 The other artists in the Yugoslav pavilion were Krsto Hegedušić, Edo Murtić, Gabrijel Stupica and Drago Tršar. Jevrić's works were singled out for admiration, including by Giorgio de Chirico, Alain Jouffroy, Enrico Crispolti, Giuseppe Marchiori and Herta Wescher.

5 Luciano Pistoi's important Turin gallery Galleria Notizie showed works by Francis Picabia, Josef Albers, Alexander Calder, Alberto Burri, Wols, Lucio Fontana, Jean Dubuffet, Louise Nevelson, Jackson Pollock, Jean Fautrier, Antoni Tàpies, Cy Twombly, Asger Jorn, Sam Francis, Mario Merz, Piero Manzoni and others.

6 Drian was opened in 1957 by Halima Nałęcz (1914–2008), who gave John Bellany, William Crozier, Michael Sandle, Yaacov Agam and others their first English exhibitions. Jevrić showed her sculpture there in 1961 alongside the work of two Yugoslav painters, Desa Pantelić and Zoran Mandić.

7 Workers' self-management was introduced in the early 1950s. Workers' councils co-managed

companies with company managers, making executive decisions. At the time, Yugoslavia had the highest levels of workers' rights in the world, and in the 1960s the country's GDP growth was second in the world after Japan. See Daniel Guerin, *Anarchism: From Theory to Practice*, introd. Noam Chomsky, Monthly Review Press, New York, 1970.

8   For the Henry Moore exhibition see Želimir Koščević, 'Henry Moore's Exhibition in Yugoslavia, 1955', *British Art Studies*, no.3, 2016, https://doi.org/10.17658/issn.2058-5462/issue-03/zkoscev.

9   See Martino Stierli, 'The Architecture of Socialist Yugoslavia as a Laboratory of Globalisation in the Cold War', in Martino Stierli et al., *Toward a Concrete Utopia: Architecture in Yugoslavia, 1948-1980*, exh. cat., Museum of Modern Art, New York, 2018-19.

10 See the essays by Ješa Denegri and Miško šuvaković in *Primeri apstrakne umetnosti, jedna radikalna istorija* [Abstract Art: A Radical History], exh. cat., Cvijeta Zuzorić Art Pavilion, Belgrade, 1996.

11 Interview with Olivera Janković in *Književni list* (Belgrade, 1 February 2005), quoted in Ješa Denegri, *Olga Jevrić*, Topy and Vojnoizdavački zavod, Belgrade, 2005, p.98.

12 Singular *stećak*, monolithic tombstones made between the twelfth and fifteenth centuries. Of approximately 60,000 stecci found across the former Yugoslavia, some 4,000 have been designated UNESCO World Heritage Sites.

13 Interview with Janković quoted in Denegri, *Olga Jevrić, op. cit.*, p.97.

14 One of the important characteristics of Yugoslav architecture of the 1960s, many of which took complex sculptural forms, was its exploration of the relationship between structure, space and form alongside new ways of building using prestressed concrete and prefab concrete elements.

15 The Staro Sajmište ('Old Fairground') was built in 1937 on the left bank of the river Sava. Shortly after the Second World War, the government began repairing war-damaged buildings and clearing the site of the Fair. Some buildings were turned into flats for poor families and in 1952 the Central Pavilion together with the Italian, Czechoslovakian and Turkish pavilions, were given to the Association of Serbian Visual Artists (Udruzenje Likovnih Umetnika Srbije, or ULUS) by Belgrade City Council. They turned these into studios for young artists and writers, some of whom also lived there. All the occupants were evicted between 2012 and 2016. For further information see the extensive study by Jovan Byford, *Staro sajmiste: Mesto secanja, zaborava I sporenja* [Old Fair: A Site Remembered, Forgotten, Contested], Beogradski centar za ljudska prava, Belgrade, 2011.

16 Mića Popović (1923-1996), a painter, filmmaker and exponent of Yugoslav *art informel*.

17 Jevrić travelled the United States extensively, meeting many artists, including Louise Bourgeois and Naum Gabo, the latter of whom she visited at his home and studio outside New York accompanied by the Macedonian sculptor Petar Hadži Boškov. The last few months of her stay were spent in New York City at the Cooper Union, where she made around 15 sculptures.

18 Tate has an extensive collection of Smith's works and in July 2019 formally acquired nine small works by Jevrić.

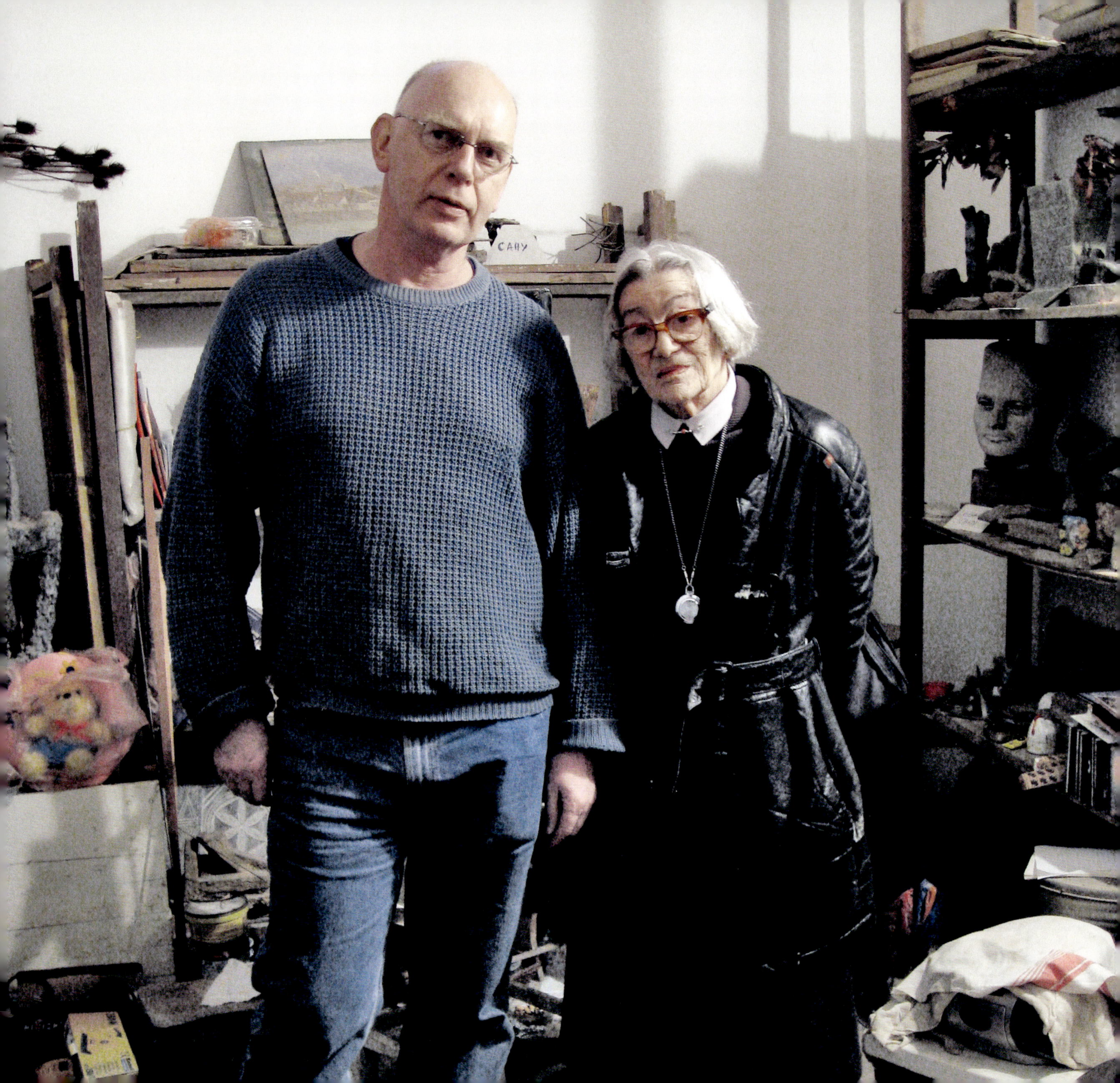

A Wonderful Artist

Richard Deacon

I have been visiting Belgrade regularly since 2006 – in part to teach at the Academy of Fine Arts, but mostly because I have been working on an ambitious project for a pedestrian bridge with my friend and colleague Mrdjan Bajić. I saw sculptures by Olga Jevrić on my first visit to the city and since then have been enriched and excited by the continuing revelations of an extraordinary body of work by a wonderful artist. Sadly, Olga died in 2014; however I did have the pleasure of meeting her on several occasions and also of visiting her studio, as well as the extraordinary collection of her works that she donated to the Serbian Academy of Sciences and Arts in 2007.

In April 2006 I was invited to the Belgrade Academy of Fine Arts as guest professor in the context of the school's exchange programme with the École Nationale Supérieure des Beaux-Arts in Paris, where I was then a professor. My host was the artist Mrdjan Bajić, who had spent a week with me in Paris the previous December as part of the same exchange programme. I had an intense week of teaching – Mrdjan's students were an engaged and talented group of committed individuals. I ran a series of open and lively seminars discussing their individual works. Talking with Mrdjan over coffee at the beginning of the visit, he bemoaned the fact that both the National Museum and the Museum of Contemporary Art (a handsome 1970s building set in parkland at the conflux of the rivers Sava and Danube) were closed for refurbishment and had been for some time. It meant that his students were deprived of engagement with a vital resource – the particularities of their own rich art history. Additionally, in the post-Milošević period, following from the breakup of Yugoslavia and the disastrous war in Kosovo, travelling outside the country had become difficult for Serbian citizens. This was particularly hard on the generation to which Mrdjan's students belonged: they had grown up in the period of the breakup, and the internet was thus the source of most of their information. Mrdjan, however, had some contacts in both museums and was able to arrange a special visit for me to both places one morning before I started teaching. I was lucky, and I am still grateful to Mrdjan for this.

Richard Deacon and
Olga Jevrić in her studio,
Belgrade, 17 April 2009

The curators in the museums were very helpful and were pleased to show off their collections, particularly at the National Museum, where, looking at the collection from the Roman period, I was even given pieces of glassware to hold in my hands (terrifying) and the items from a Roman silver dinner service to feel their heft. In the sculpture collection, two bronze works caught my eye – abstract items where the lumpy elements of a fragmented whole were held in a dynamic between expansion and contraction. The rods that acted as the armatures of these dynamic assemblies could equally be thought of as being held in their particular configuration by the lumps of matter adhering to them. Intrigued, I asked the name of the artist. Olga Jevrić: I wrote it down so that I could ask Mrdjan about her. At the Museum of Contemporary Art the situation was very confused, since the storage of their collection had been moved to the upper-floor galleries after flooding in their basement and ground floor, but I did see at least one other sculpture by Jevrić – a kind of unfurling, fern-like form that reinforced my interest. When I asked Mrdjan about her on the way back to the academy, he told me that he knew her quite well and that he liked both her and the work very much.

Later in the same week, Mrdjan and I met for dinner with Ljiljana Obradović, the director of the Belgrade Fortress museum in Kalemegdan, and Marina Andrić, her deputy and chief curator. Ostensibly this was because they were seeking advice on the restoration of Ivan Meštrović's magnificent post-First World War monument in the park surrounding the fortress (acidic water leaking out from the only partially removed core of the bronze sculpture was eating into the fine bas-reliefs on the faces of the plinth). This was followed by a question as to whether I myself might be interested in proposing a sculpture of my own, for a site of my choosing in the park. Naturally this was an interesting invitation; however, I told them that, to me, it would be even more interesting if I could work with an artist based in Belgrade on some sort of collaborative project – and further said that I hoped Mrdjan would be interested in this idea. I knew his work somewhat and had come to respect him hugely from our working together at the art schools in Paris and Belgrade – I thought we would get on. To my delight, he accepted the offer. I now knew that I would be returning to Belgrade and, among other things, that I would have the chance to discover more of the work of Olga Jevrić.

The first return was in September 2006 – quite a short visit, mainly concentrated on spending time in Kalemegdan and thinking about how the two of us were going to work together and what we might do. Mrdjan and I met again in Paris in 2007 by then we had each begun to think about something which eventually became the pedestrian bridge, *From There to Here*. In 2008 we began to work intensively on the project and I made three extended visits to Belgrade. During the first of these, in July, Mrdjan told me that Olga Jevrić had installed a group of her smaller sculptures in her academician's room at the Serbian Academy of Sciences and Arts and was happy to receive visitors there. The academy was just around the corner from where we were working (a building that was an annex of the art school), so, of course, we went to visit. Her room was on the third floor of the imposing building, which obviously contained many similar rooms,

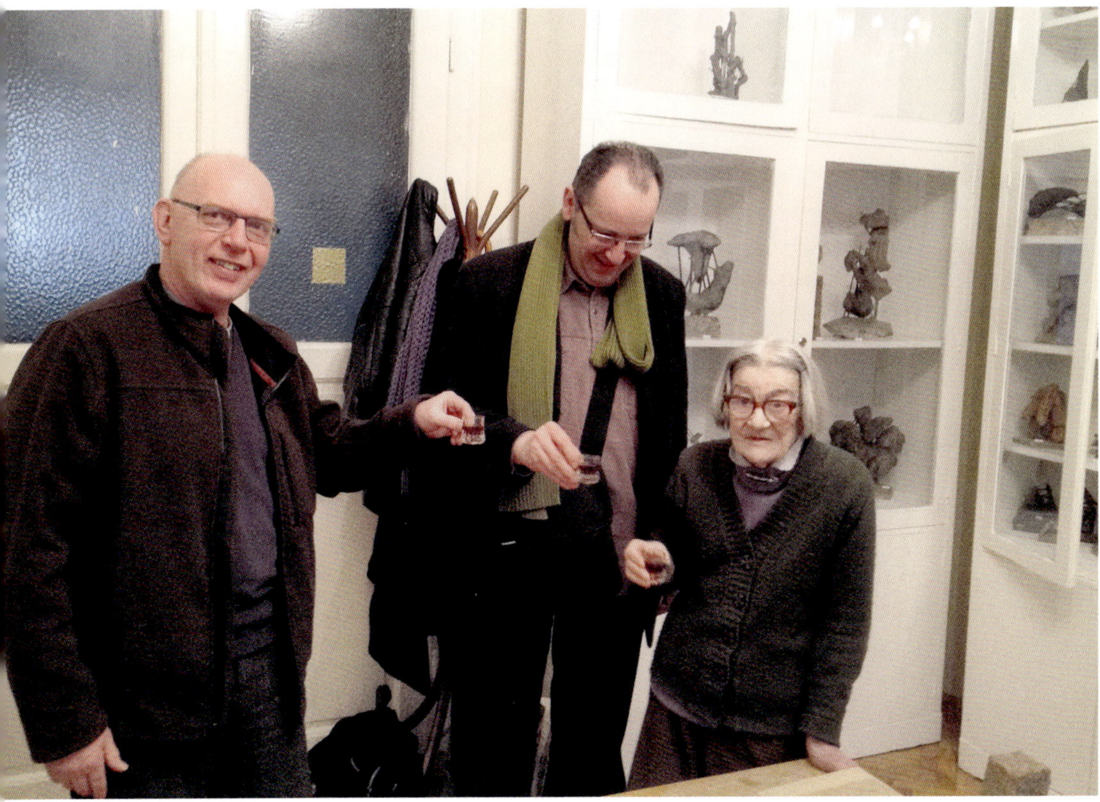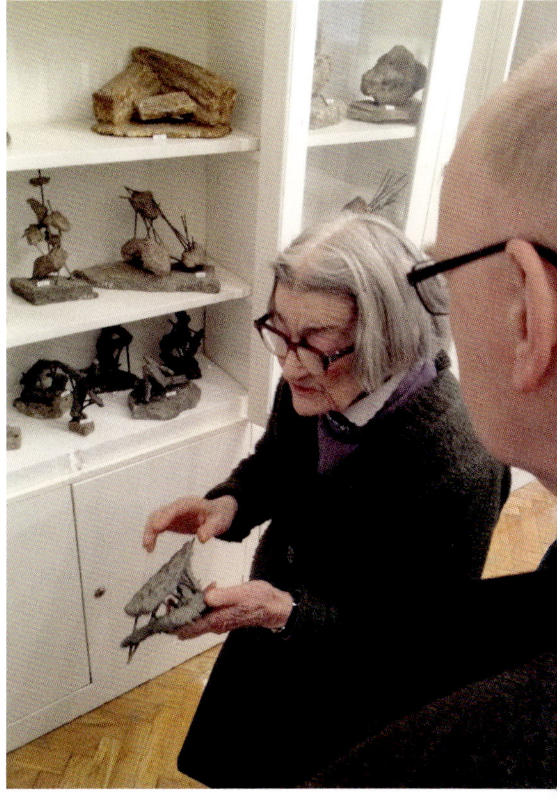

their closed doors visible along long corridors like some hotel for intellectuals, none giving an indication as to their contents (latterly Olga's room did have a sculpture on a low pedestal outside the door). The room was not large, perhaps 5 × 4 metres, with a window in the wall opposite the door and the walls otherwise lined with glass-fronted bookcase cabinets. Olga sat at a table near the door, a petite, grey-haired, lively woman wearing strong glasses that magnified her eyes. Having made the introductions, Mrdjan talked with Olga, allowing me to walk slowly around the room. There were six shelves in the cabinets on the sides of the room and, at the back, behind the table where Olga was sitting, a slightly deeper cabinet with three shelves, double height between them. Arrayed on the shelves were 147 small sculptures, mostly made from a mixture of plaster or concrete containing iron oxide, and iron rods or large nails, some set on small bases of various materials. Seeing this extraordinary assemblage together was an incredibly intense

Richard Deacon, Mrdjan Bajić and Olga Jevrić in her room at the Serbian Academy of Sciences and Arts, 13 March 2009

and deeply memorable sculptural experience. In part this was because of the contrast between the room and the institutional anonymity of the lifts and corridors outside, but mostly because of the works, spanning a focused working life of 60 years. Of the works in the collection, the first, a cast concrete relief from 1948, was the only cast; the rest were all individually constructed, some serving as models or proposals for larger works, but all combining an implicit monumentality with a highly specific material structure. They were thus, individually, highly contained yet potentially much larger – an explosive combination. Each was numbered, with a small paper number either glued or taped to the base or placed onto the shelf beside the work. Although the inventory catalogue of this collection reveals this numbering to be chronological (the concrete cast being number 1) and the sequence in the room vaguely followed chronology – with the earliest on the left as you came into the room, then advancing clockwise to the most recent on the right, towards the door – other factors were also in play. Most obviously, the larger-spaced shelves at the back held the tallest works. There were other groupings too, either to do with size (as at the back) or common motif. In some cases there were particularly play-offs between individual works and the others in the group on a shelf. This arrangement was clearly deliberate. At some point I began asking questions, and Olga removed a small work to show me something or other about how it was made.

In working with plaster, Olga Jevrić habitually added a quantity of ferric oxide to the mix. This gives the plaster a rusty surface and serves both to strengthen the material and to make it easier to bond additional wet plaster to dried components or to bond two previously formed lumps together. Iron rods (or large nails) might serve as a kind of armature, bound together by lumps of plaster (*Emanation 1*, 1970/83) or to separate lumps so that a composite whole could seem slightly expanded (*Centripetal Form 1*, 1964/65). In a few works these rods, by being installed parallel to each other, form planes or screens (*Weaving through Space*, 1969/78). A space between two lumps could be charged by the dynamism of the interconnecting rods (*Aggressive Forms 1*, 1959). Iron rods could spray out of a lump like sparks from a fire (*Hiatus 1a*, 1967/73). In the works from the 1980s and 1990s these rods and lumps become subsumed into sets of block – or beam-like forms, roughly square in section with scarified surfaces and doing double duty for both rod and lump (*Permeation 1*, 1986, *Gredna II*, 1996).

In the room itself, the intensity of reflection (not at all programmatic) on the emotional content of solid and void through the use of really quite simple materials was inspirational, and a powerful introduction to a body of work by an artist who I thought really should be better known. In part, however, this was a reflection of my own ignorance, as well as of the vicissitudes of global and regional politics: Olga Jevrić was not an unknown artist – her very membership of the Serbian Academy of Sciences and Arts attests to that. She had major exhibitions in Serbia and former Yugoslavia and held gallery shows in Turin and London. From the early 1950s she took part in many group exhibitions internationally. In 1958, at the 29th Venice Biennale, she made a substantive showing in the Yugoslav pavilion. She travelled extensively, including, in 1966, spending a year in the US on a Ford Foundation Fellowship, crossing the country and meeting many artists.

Those two weeks in Belgrade in 2008 went very well, and I was to return twice more the same year. Mrdjan and I formulated a plan for a pedestrian bridge linking the burgeoning waterfront of the river Sava to Belgrade Fortress, crossing a railway and a dual carriageway that posed significant barriers for access, and incorporating a lift tower that supported a sculpture combining elements by the two of us. We worked to scale on a large topographical model that Fedja Klikovac had secured funding for through the Henry Moore Foundation. It was fun, and by the end of the year much of the design was worked out. I had also visited Olga in her studio, a very different, much darker space compared to that room in the academy, and had expressed my desire to her to try and find a way to bring an exhibition of her work to London. I returned many times to Belgrade over the years as the bridge project developed (or didn't!) and visited Olga often but I never fulfilled that ambition. The best I could achieve in her lifetime was to show a group of three larger sculptures in a group show at the Ludwig Museum in Koblenz. The tireless efforts of Fedja Klikovac and Ingrid Swenson have enabled this substantial solo exhibition to take place, and I hope that a London audience can begin to appreciate what a wonderful artist Olga Jevrić was.

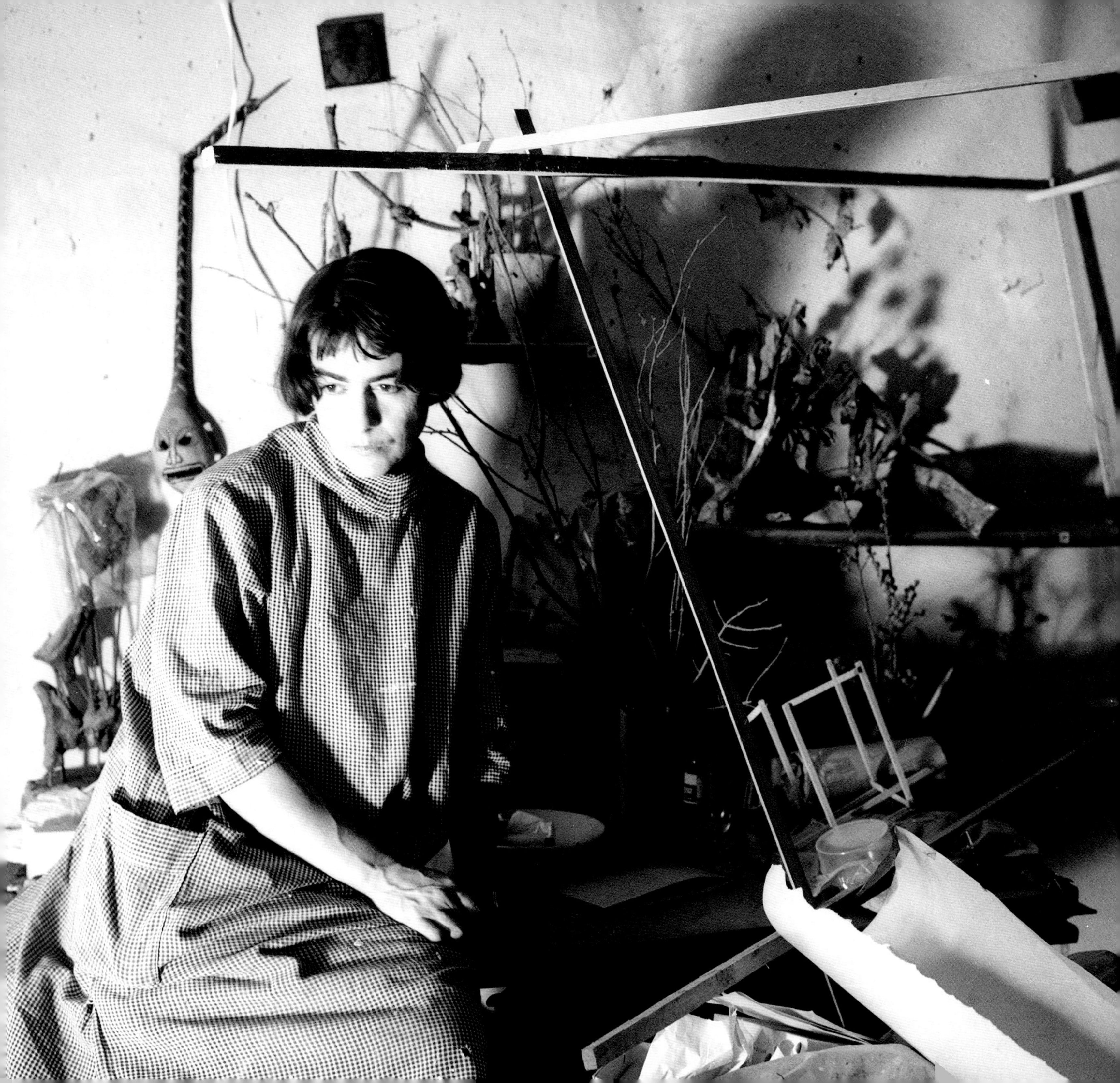

in her own time

Phyllida Barlow

'… like eating something that is not often on the menu …'
Melanie Counsell, after seeing the Olga Jevrić exhibition at PEER, July 2019

night and day
cold and hot
hard and soft
open and shut
full and empty
still and moving
rough and smooth
silence and noise
fast and slow

the list is endless, and banal –
but despite their banality, opposites can be pertinent;
and there is always the well-known maxim that opposites attract;
and they can become complicated:

what are the 'opposites' to such everyday things
as a tree, the sky, a chair or a tennis racket –
which 'opposites' do these singular things attract?
and even more subtle is whether there can be opposites for such conditions
as a reverie, the sound of humming, or the emotion of hurt feelings –
do these require descriptions to identify what their exact qualities are
in order to discover their opposites?
or do these conditions not have opposites?

but everything has an opposite, doesn't it?
so maybe associations and comparisons become significant
in capturing the sense of what the opposites might be
of emotional, psychological or physical conditions:
is the opposite of 'pain' simply 'pain-free', or 'painless'?
but these are 'opposites' that only emphasise the condition of 'pain',

Olga Jevrić in her studio,
Staro sajmište, Belgrade,
c.1960s

offering nothing about what the state of being 'pain-free' or 'painlessness' might be;
and can the conditions of being 'pain-free' and 'painless'
only be experienced when there has been pain?

describing the particularities of pain therefore
becomes essential in order to discover its opposite –
those who suffer from persistent pain
talk about being imprisoned by it,
its unrelenting presence,
a phantom state, but all too real and grotesque;
pain is monotonous, cruel, devouring, incapacitating, menacing,
and all of these can play with similes:
pain is like being imprisoned, and being devoured,
like a menace from an unknown source, as is its cruelty –
always a threat, which incapacitates;
and being imprisoned by pain implies an unjust incarceration
without reason

but why this perusal of 'opposites'
when the subject of this writing is the sculpture of Olga Jevrić?

the simple answer is that Jevrić's work
is construed around the most beguiling,
but potentially brutal, of opposites:
flesh and bone;
and why would flesh and bone be considered opposites?
each needs the other:
the bone requires the flesh to make movement possible
while the flesh needs the bone for support;
one is hard, rigid and structural, the other soft, flexible, mutable;
the attraction between these opposites is harmonic,
and each becomes dysfunctional without the other;

Olga Jevrić was a sculptor, born in 1922 in Beograd, Serbia, where she died in 2014;
an artist who has been a well-kept secret;
the brutal cultural gagging by political regimes, the strife of civil wars,
destabilised economies and numerous other Eurocentric complexities
have hidden so many artists across Europe,
and Olga Jevrić is one such artist;

however, thanks to the dedicated collaboration of
Fedja Klikovac of Handel Street Projects, Richard Deacon,
the Olga Jevrić Estate in Serbia and Ingrid Swenson of PEER,
this extraordinary artist's work is now seeing the light of day;

Jevrić has a focused sculptural vocabulary,
obsessively and repetitively fusing structure and mass;
the materials are consistent –
steel rods are welded, brazed and bound at intersections
to construct basic, upright and horizontal structures;
the steel rods are interrupted by forms modelled
from a compound of cement and ferric oxide,
and these modelled lumps and shapes carry the touch of the maker herself,
as if emerging from the stroke and grasp of a cupped hand,
forms that could be being impaled by the rods
or could be hugging and clinging to these structural elements;
there is both certainty and uncertainty
here is the powerful combination of flesh and bone,
but with none of the literal connotations that such naming implies:
there is no flesh and no bone
but these works reverberate with the fragility of the exposed flayed body,
whether that be as metaphor or as memory,
whether that be rooted in war-damaged and devastated buildings and humanity
or in the dreadful state of aftermath,
all of which is redeemed in the raw beauty of these works
where deep, dark pain is given compelling new life through simple acts of making,
through the bone of steel and the flesh of rust-impregnated cement;

the works in the exhibitions
at PEER and Handel Street Projects
are all small in size,
the largest work measuring approximately 120 centimetres high,
but their size belies their potential scale:
although complete and succinct as they are,
these works harbour a sense of enormity,
particularly with the small block sculptures
where the scratched, rugged cement and ferric oxide slabs
are perilously balanced, or forcefully erect, or lie casually recumbent,

as if fallen randomly;
and although performing as models
the block sculptures beg to be experienced as structures and forms
that interact with our own physical size –
to rise above us, prompting us to reconsider
our relationship to them and the world around, natural and human-made;

but the small size of these works emphasises
the intensity of the acts of making
that have brought them into existence

the various elements
that comprise many of the sculptures in both exhibition venues
are hand-sized and evidence the squeeze of fingers and palm;
the immediacy of how the materials have been handled is urgent
and very much in the present:
these works could have been made today;

the compression inherent to the forms
in both the rod and lump works and the block works
provokes an unease,
and, as mentioned,
questions arise as to whether
the skeletal steel rods and long nail structures,
which protrude erratically from the pressed shapes
of the rod and lump sculptures,
are stabbed into the cement and ferric oxide lumps, trapping them,
or whether these lumps are squeezed around the rods, clinging on, as if about to slip –
are these forms, which are so fixed by the rods and nails, in fact on the move,
about to escape and break out of their incarceration?
or are they protected by their steel framework
and therefore settled where they are?
this uncertainty is at the heart of the work
and is its invisible centre –
an emotion rather than a subject;

the larger works, which extend beyond the hand-held
and are between 30 and 120 centimetres in height, also carry this hot immediacy,
and the larger size enables the mechanics of the works to be fully appreciated;

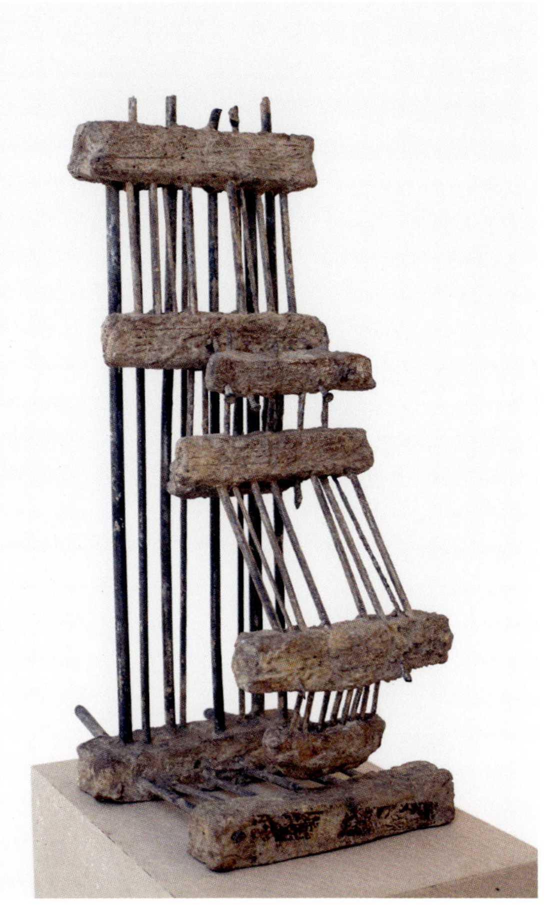

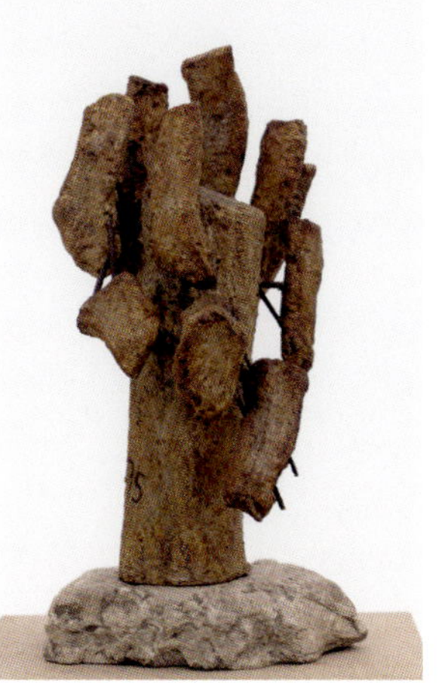

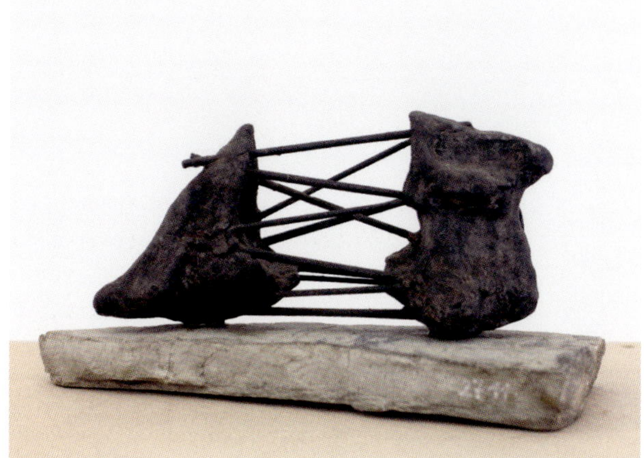

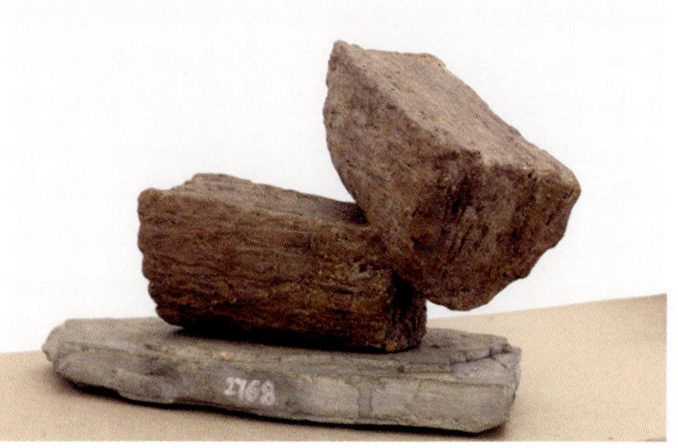

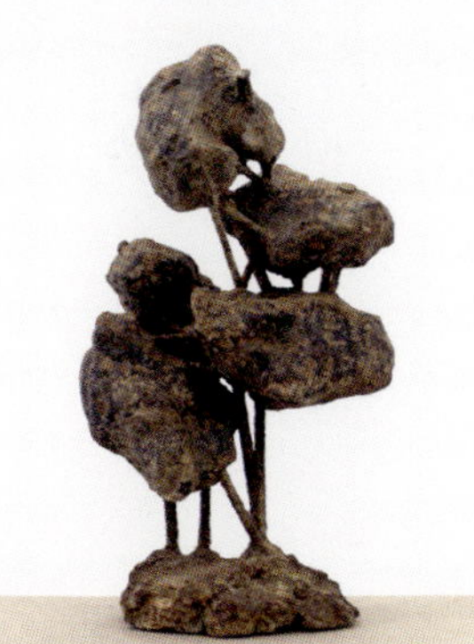

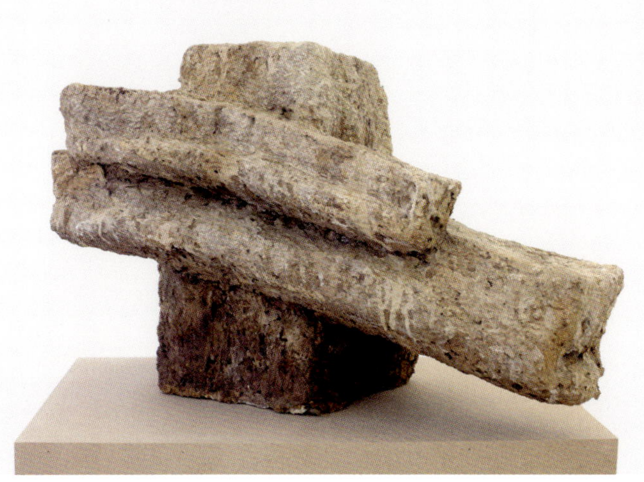

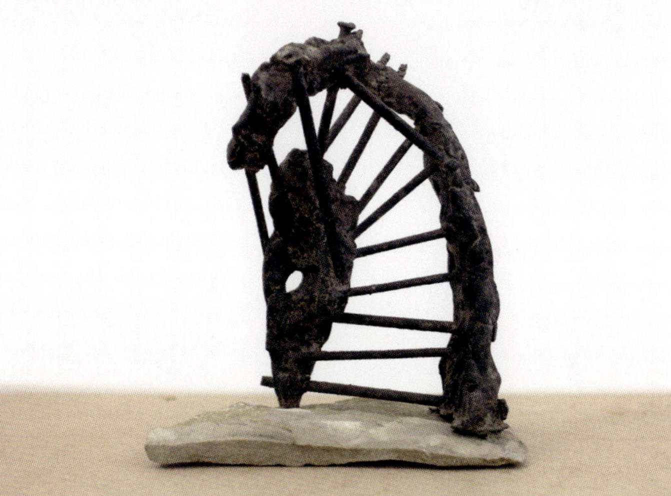

empty spaces, opened up by the fretwork of steel rods
and accompanying cement and ferric oxide lumps,
are danced around by the pushing, pulling, balancing, protruding, tumbling, catching
of the forms as they embrace or are impaled on the lethal rods and nails;
the daylight that punctures these works deceives:
lumps become thrown, landing as if by chance,
emphasising spontaneity, improvisation and anti-form characteristics
with an effortless ease,
and the bright, gaping empty spaces
become as substantial as the lumps themselves;

there is a simplicity in the language
but a subtle complexity in how the works achieve contradictions:
the rhythmic tossing and turning of the mass of the lumps is bewitching;
flames of an open fire command the same restless fascination:
no sooner is a pattern discerned in the flames than it disappears…
an Olga Jevrić work mesmerises in a similar way –
searching for where the centre of a work might be
leads us into a flickering world of visceral surfaces
folding inwards, outwards, around and through,
and although trapped into the stillness of sculpture,
these works seduce and lure their viewers into an uncanny quest of looking,
an act that has no final resting place

our physical act of looking and searching
is given a different focus with the block works –
majestic arrangements of chunks of the cement and ferric oxide compound;
if these are sedentary objects then their stillness competes
with their relationship to light, dark, weight and gravity;
the airborne juggling of the steel rod and lump sculptures
has been transformed into collisions
of light-filled and dark-shadowed surfaces,
manipulating the innate solidity and mass of the resulting blocks;
upright and stern, recumbent and indolent, leaning and thrusting,
these blocks also have a simplicity in their sculptural language,
and a complexity:
their obvious desire to become huge monumental works is clear,
but as small nameless objects

they are defiant in their obstinate ambiguity,
claiming an indefinable identity,
refuting both the natural and the human-made world;

May 2019, Beograd, Serbia,
a civic building,
a typical institutional building,
columned, with a flight of steps
up and down which students are coming and going –
maybe a university building, a library perhaps

inside, it's down four flights of stairs,
past closed doors concealing corridors and rooms,
then arriving in a basement,
and another corridor, disappearing into darkness,
lined on both sides with stacks of books,
paperbacks, dust covered, dormant;
an occasional title or name fleetingly appears:
Freud and his Masters…, *Derrida: Reconsidering His…*, *…Aristotelian…*'

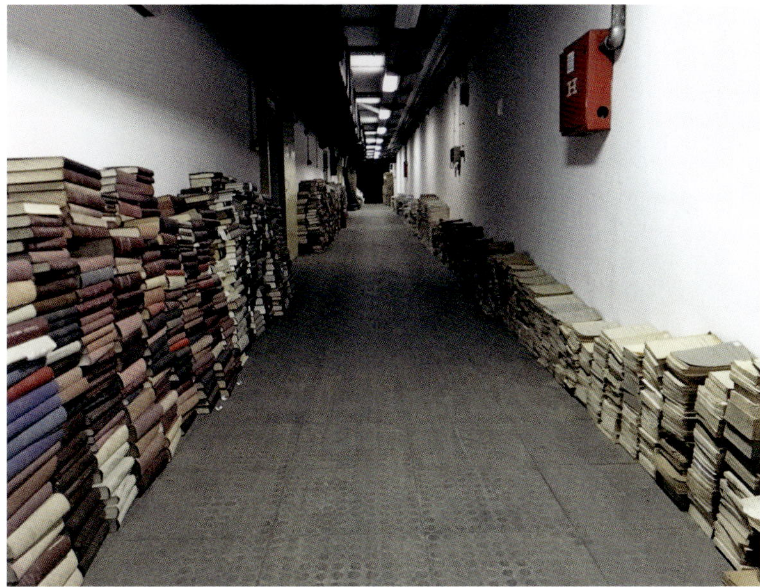

Basement of the Svetozar
Marković University
Library, Belgrade, 2019

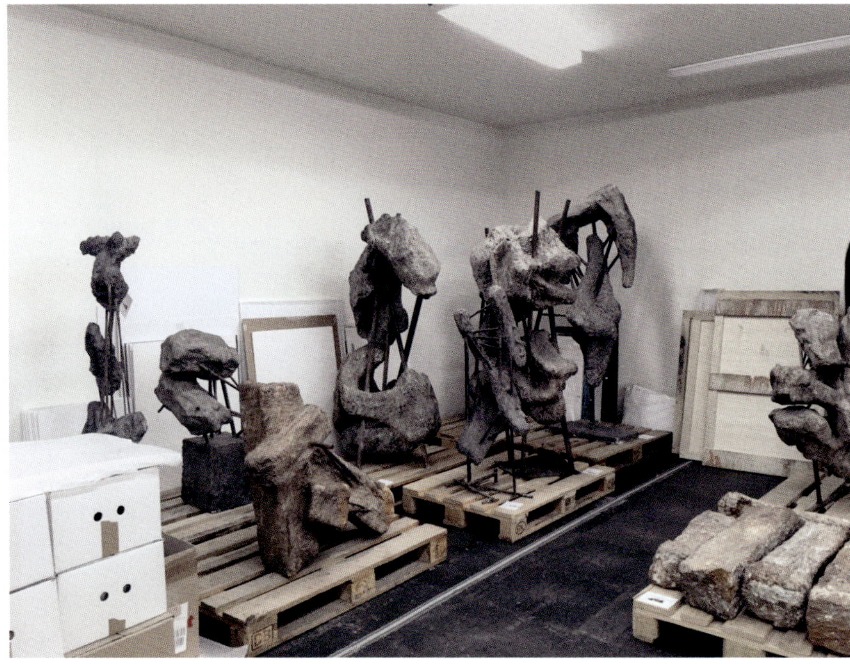

Heritage House art storage, basement of the Svetozar Marković University Library, Belgrade, 2019

the corridor narrows and opens up into a room, brightly lit,
with a low ceiling bisected by large galvanised air vents;
it is a room that functions as a storage space;
stashed at one end, expediently and unprotected, huddled together,
some thirty sculptures by the deceased artist Olga Jevrić;

at first, it is a heap, squatted on palettes on the floor –
the uniformity of colour is bewildering: muted greys, pinks and rust reds;
each work merges into the next,
an organic mass, abandoned and almost akin to debris;
gradually the works reveal themselves as entities…
a folded form, suspended but pierced by a steel rod, attracts my attention;
it conceals other lumps and bumps, also pierced by steel rods;
it is beguiling in its directness and simple construction;
I am intrigued by these qualities – they are familiar,
I know I have seen something like this before…

and another work distinguishes itself,
a barely touched, but modelled, cement carapace, hollowed out,
shielding a regiment of nails, sharp ends upwards –
a brutal, raw and protecting object;

other works offer themselves,
and soon I am thoroughly engrossed;

I am back in the early 1960s
introducing myself to the contemporary sculpture of that time;
I am deeply involved and intrigued;
it is a steep but compelling learning curve
as I look at Richier and discover Louise Nevelson
and of course Picasso's sculpture;
Jean Arp, Naum Gabo, Henri Laurens;
there are many others,
and a lot of cumbersome European sculpture,
and Americans,
in particular David Smith, whose work is a difficult inspiration;
I look further afield
and stumble upon the Gutai group, Meret Oppenheim, César, Zadkine, Wotruba…

the diversity is both thrilling and disconcerting –
where do I fit in? where are the women? are all acts of making the same,
from fixing together a bicycle wheel and a stool,
to modelling swollen female forms?
how to choose, and how not to choose?

at that time, I browse my books on sculpture,
black-and-white photographs, numerous images,
many male sculptors,
a range of materials but mostly bronze and stone;
the solid and massive and the open-framed and elegant…

but by 1963 the sculptureness of what I was feeding upon begins to pall;

the mid-1960s come to the rescue –
Arte povera emerges in the UK, along with land art, and art made beyond the studio, from the USA and Europe,
and numerous interpretations of those movements
that eschewed the previous sculptural beliefs of the 1940s, 1950s and early 1960s;

in the basement with the stored Jevrić works
I reminisce to myself about the sculptural language
I so vehemently rejected in the early 1960s,
having been so enamoured by it when I first began to make sculpture;
and now, laid out before me, was all that that language espoused,
and I was again profoundly moved by it and what it stands for:
its wordlessness, its intense formalism
where different postures claim such different emotional motives –
vertical versus folded, horizontal versus vertical, diagonal versus suspended…
and the traces of making are revealed, the fragility of incompleteness,
the timing of when to stop, the rawness of the materiality and physicality,
the provisional acts of fixing and joining, the economy of touch,
the unstoppable improvisations…

back to May 2019, and back in London,
I get out my old books on sculpture:
Michel Seuphor's *The Sculpture of this Century*,
Jean Selz's *Modern Sculpture: Origins and Evolution*
and
Carola Giedion-Welcker's *Contemporary Sculpture: An Evolution in Volume and Space* –
they all date back to the late 1950s and early 1960s;

although astounded and moved by seeing and experiencing Olga Jevrić's work
in the basement storage space,
and shocked by its powerful presence and distinctive identity,
I am also bewildered by how comfortable I am with it
because it is so familiar to me;
it is as if I had always known the work
and am able to experience it with clarity and total empathy;

on the cover of Giedion-Welker's book
is an image that resonates:
a black-and-white image showing an elongated modelled form, cast in bronze, suspended in the centre of a cage,
densely constructed from thin rods welded to form overlapping triangular frames;
the apexes of the triangles thrust upwards, pleadingly,
while the recumbent form trapped in the centre is both imprisoned and protected;
the work is titled *Model for the Monument to the Unknown Political Prisoner*,
1955, bronze, by Luciano Minguzzi

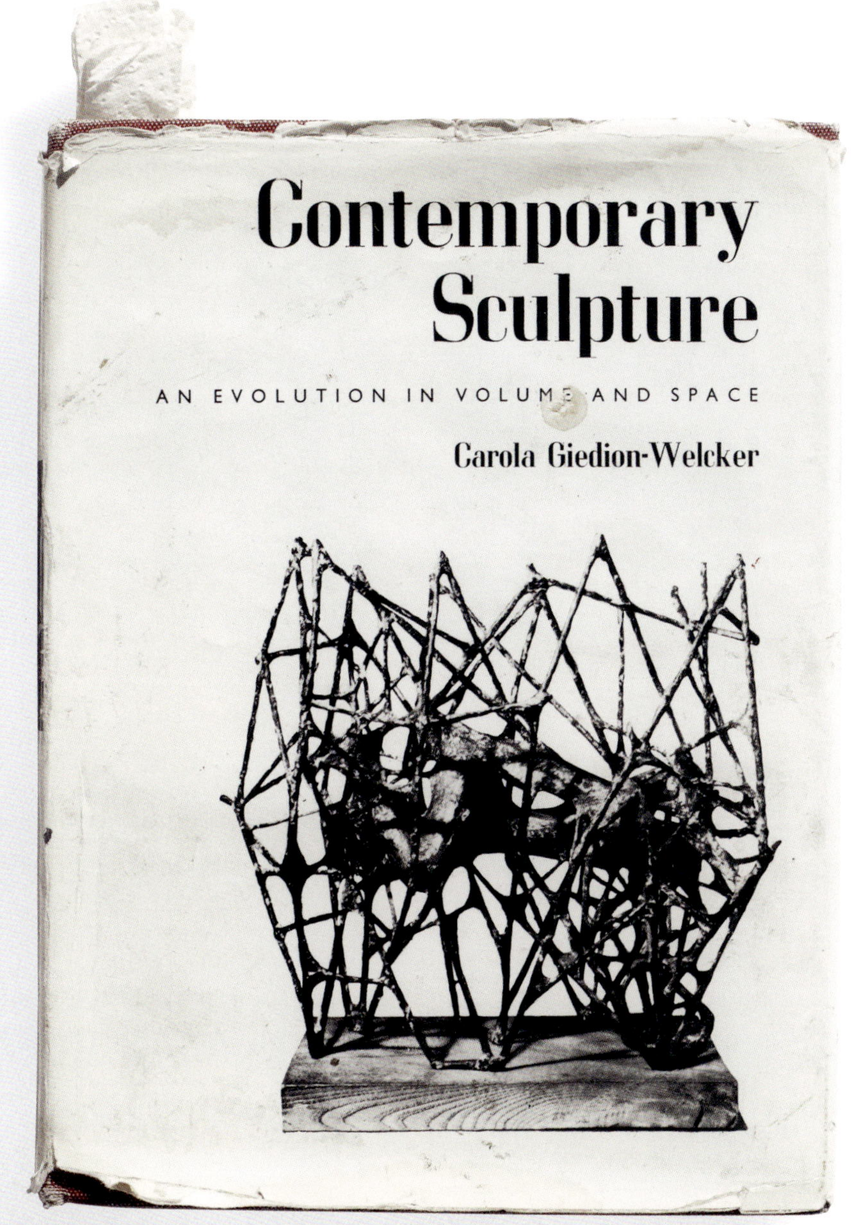

Phyllida Barlow's copy of
Carola Giedion-Welcker's
*Contemporary Sculpture: An
Evolution in Volume and Space*,
Faber & Faber, 1960

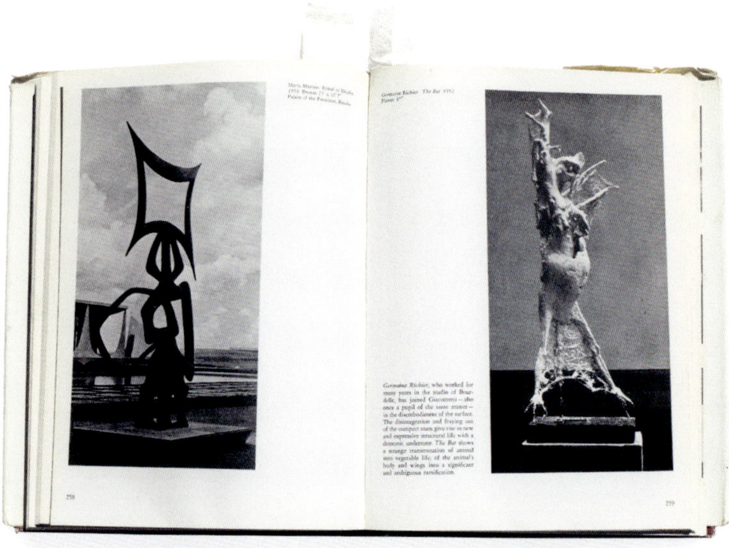

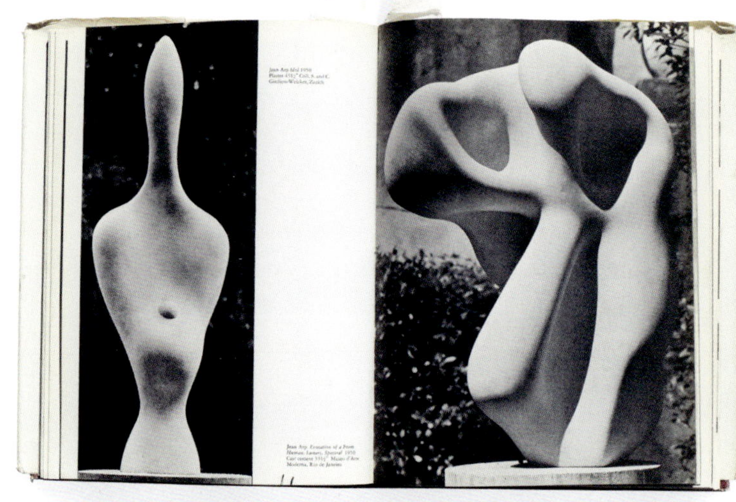

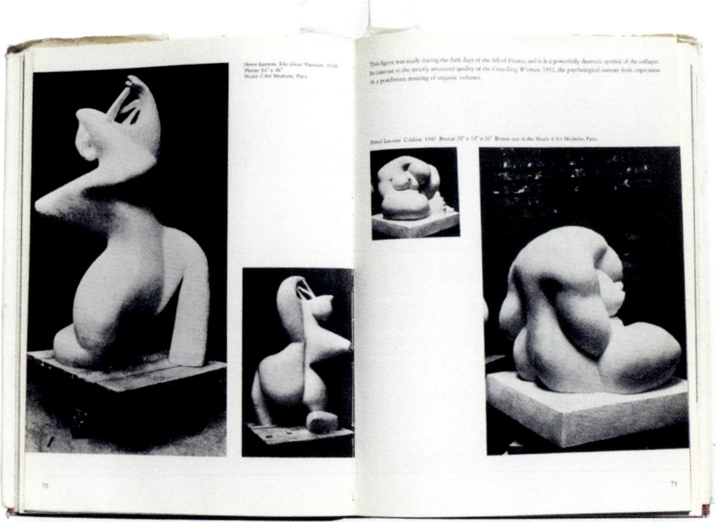

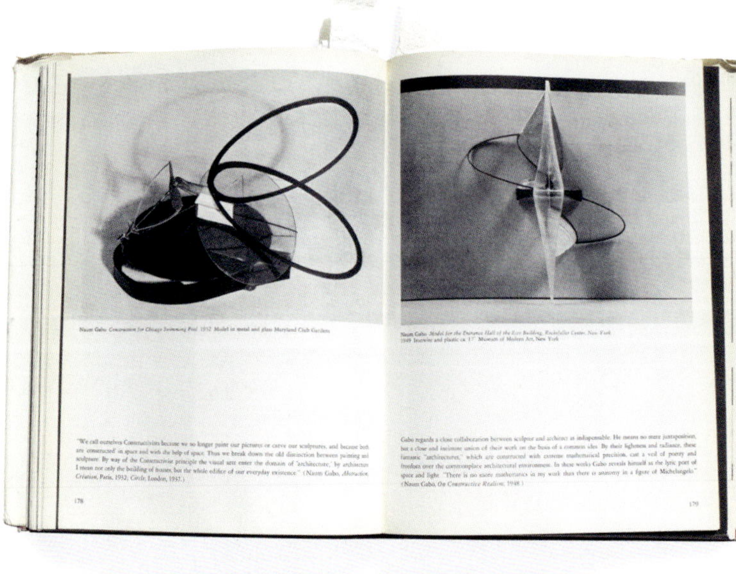

for me, Jevrić's work is contextualised by the remarkable sculpture
that emerged before, during and after the Second World War,
reflecting the violence, destruction and cruelty
that the world was being plunged into;

the formal, intellectual, aesthetic and conceptual concerns
that ranged from the impact of Duchamp and the readymade,
through to the highly skilled, compressed masses of dense carvings
that reveal imaginative adventures into invented form,
and on to the spatial experiments with transparency, frames and grids
that opened up sculpture to gravity, light and time –
these provide the background to Jevrić's extraordinary body of work,
lying dormant in the library basement in Beograd;

Jevrić is referenced in Seuphor's book –
the work illustrated is *Project for a Monument* from 1956,
utilising both an open framework of steel rods and the mass of modelled cement,
and even though it is a small work it somehow embraces sculpture's then concerns;

now, visiting the exhibitions at PEER and Handel Street Projects,
this relationship with a history of sculpture
in which I was so immersed in the early 1960s
disappears

released from its basement store
and installed in the two exhibition venues,
Jevrić's sculpture takes on its true powerful significance:

Olga Jevrić's space-hungry works now have the space to stand alone,
and the demands that each work makes for the space it requires are fulfilled;
light and air flow through these works
revealing their visceral potency, their deeply personal singularity
and, above all, their opposing forces:
their uncanny relevance to the troubled times we live in now,
reciprocated by their awkward beauty and enlightening physical presence;
an embodiment of hope and despair, and despair and hope;
a timeless affirmation that opposites do attract.

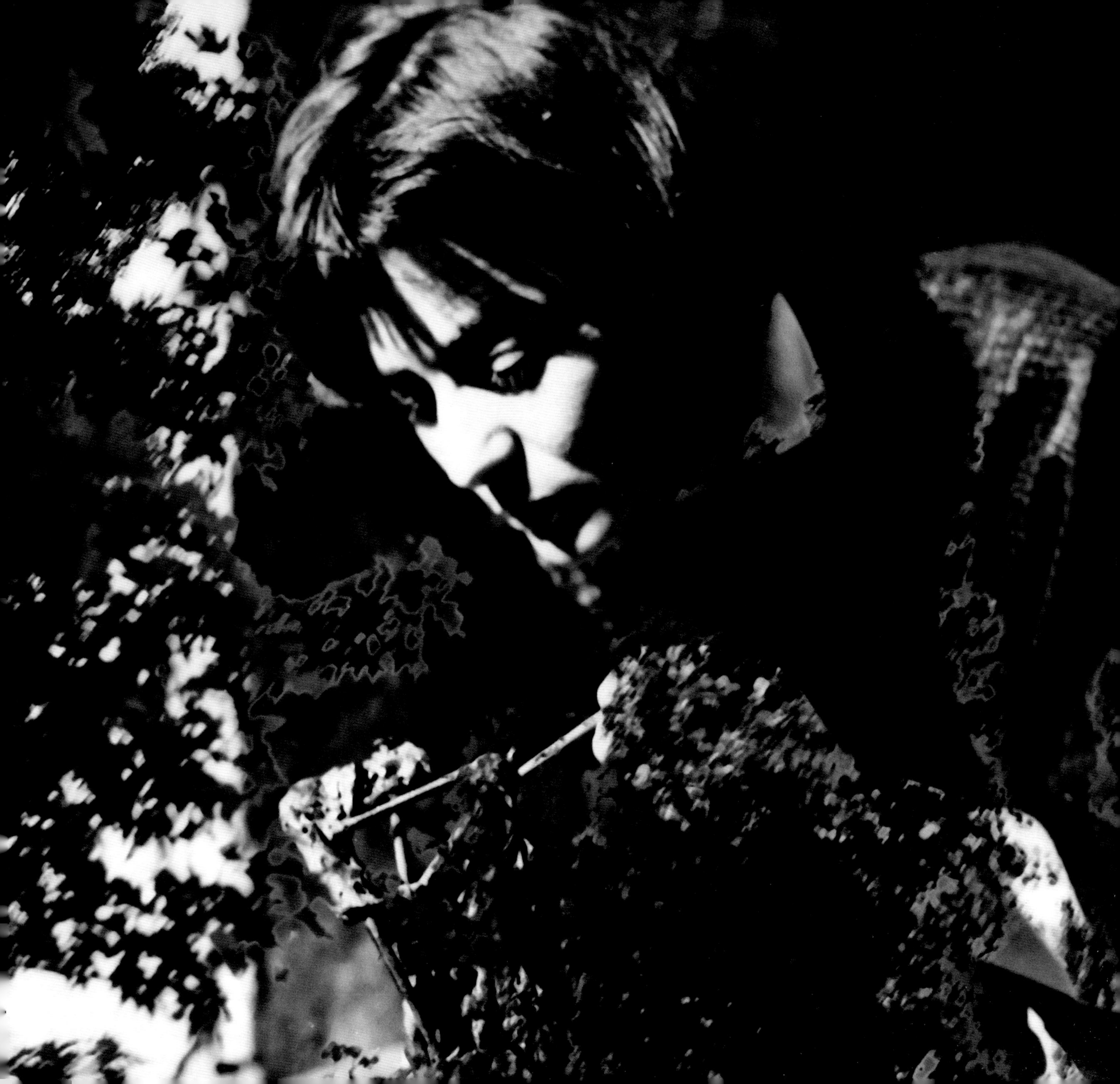

Olga Jevrić

Ješa Denegri

Olga Jevrić's sculpture is well known, thoroughly researched and held in high esteem in her homeland.[1] Born in 1922, Jevrić graduated from the Belgrade Academy of Music in 1946 and two years later from the Academy of Fine Arts, after which she received a Master's degree in art history from the faculty of philosophy of the University of Belgrade. Her academic background is particularly notable and points indirectly to the character of her sculpture: her purist, abstract sculptural language can be regarded as relating directly to her study and knowledge of music. After nearly ten years of taking part in group exhibitions, and her first solo exhibition at Belgrade's ULUS Gallery in 1957, when she was working in a more traditional figurative style, Jevrić's new, abstract sculptural language signalled a significant development in contemporary art in Serbia. As a result of her participation in the 29th Venice Biennale in 1958, where her work was acclaimed by significant European critics, she had her first solo exhibition outside Yugoslavia the following year, at Luciano Pistoi's Notizie Gallery in Turin, and a three-person exhibition at Halima Nałęcz's Drian Galleries in

Olga Jevrić in the garden of her studio, Staro Sajmište, Belgrade, 1957

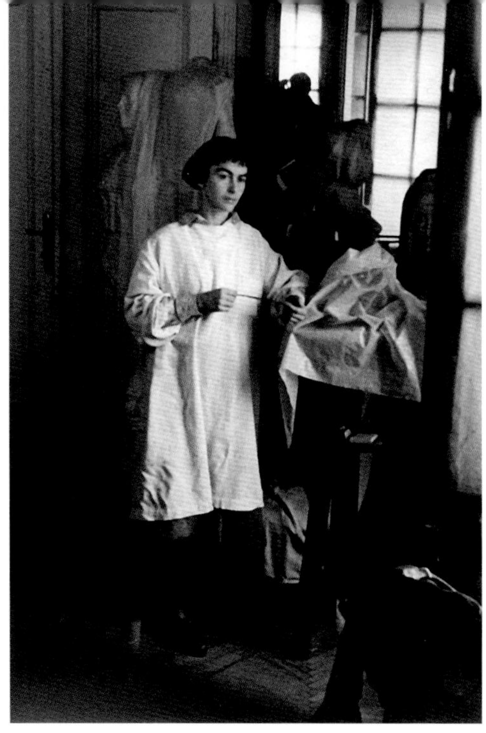

left Olga Jevrić, Belgrade, 1951

below Olga Jevrić, London, 1961–2

London (1962). Retrospective exhibitions followed in Belgrade at the Museum of Contemporary Art (1981) and on a smaller scale at SKC Gallery (at the Student Cultural Centre; 1988), the Gallery of the Serbian Academy of Sciences and Arts (2001) and Heritage House (2012).

Jevrić's formative style developed in the first postwar decade, in the context of the officially sanctioned Socialist realist style, which developed as the Soviet government began to loosen its strictures, gradually opening to Western art and eventually breaking with the ideology. Although Jevric's academic instruction would have been only modestly informed by developments of modern sculpture, some of her remarkable early portraits such as *Portrait of Angelina Gatalica* (1952–53) stand out in their capacity for self-contained sculptural reflection. Rather than assimilating the domestic sculptural heritage of the interwar period that was handed down by her art school instructors, Jevrić turned towards conceptualising the language of sculpture, sparked by

her awareness of essentially different artistic and cultural sources. The Belgrade-based artist Petar Lubarda (1907–1974) played a formative role in encouraging her development; she found the robust forms in his paintings alongside his non-descriptive use of paint instructive. Lubarda's 1951 exhibition at ULUS Gallery was for her specifically influential in terms of his claim to the free communication of his ideas. Visits to the Venice Biennale in 1952 and 1954 and study trips to Paris and London in 1955, as well as the seminal exhibition of contemporary American art in Belgrade in 1956, featuring leading Abstract Expressionist artists, significantly contributed to the formation of Jevrić's views on the nature of contemporary formal and operative artistic processes, in tune with the conceptual and psychological predispositions of the artists of the first postwar generation.

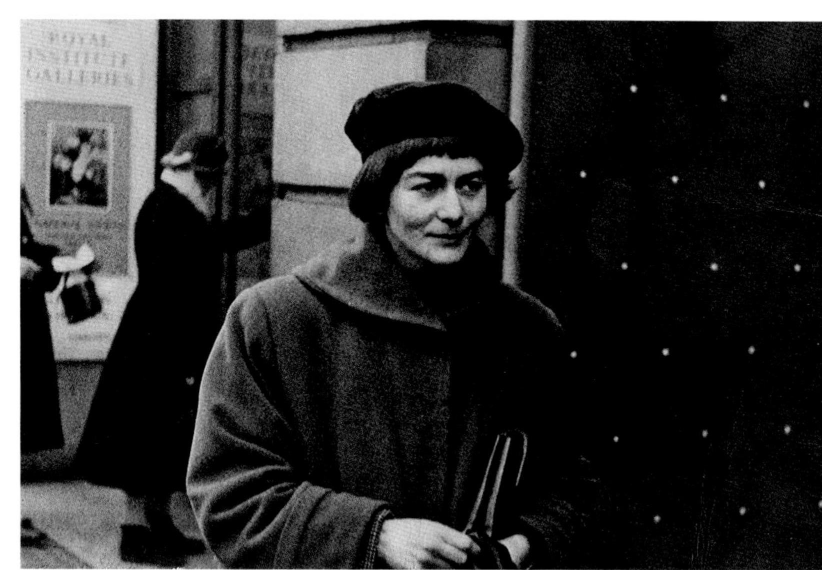

On occasions she gave poignant testimonies of her own experience and of the sentiments of other members of her generation, not only as artists but as humans:

The war and postwar circumstances have brought destruction and collective suffering. My generation is overwhelmed – as a witness or participant – with content that has been imposed as a condition, a reason for creativity. Our reflections were not a response to a commission. They resulted from a need for catharsis, as a debt to those who no longer exist – as identification through a sign.[2]

And elsewhere:

In my opinion, a monument is a sanctuary, a secularised temple. It implies the existence of an external and internal structure. The external structure has an invoking-sign function, whereas the internal has the function of emphasising values that suggest respect for the spirits of those who perished in the name of those same values.[3]

These passages clearly demonstrate Jevrić's initial and basic motivation for choosing her path as a sculptor was to take on the challenge of creating a memorial for her times. It was in this context that she conceived the first *Proposal for a Monument* (for Prokuplje, Serbia) in 1951, and the subsequent *Proposal for a Monument – Milanovac* in 1954. Many others followed with the same basic title but without specified locations (several were made as entries to competitions, and despite being awarded on several occasions, the works were never realised). Such proposals for monuments, dedicated to nameless victims

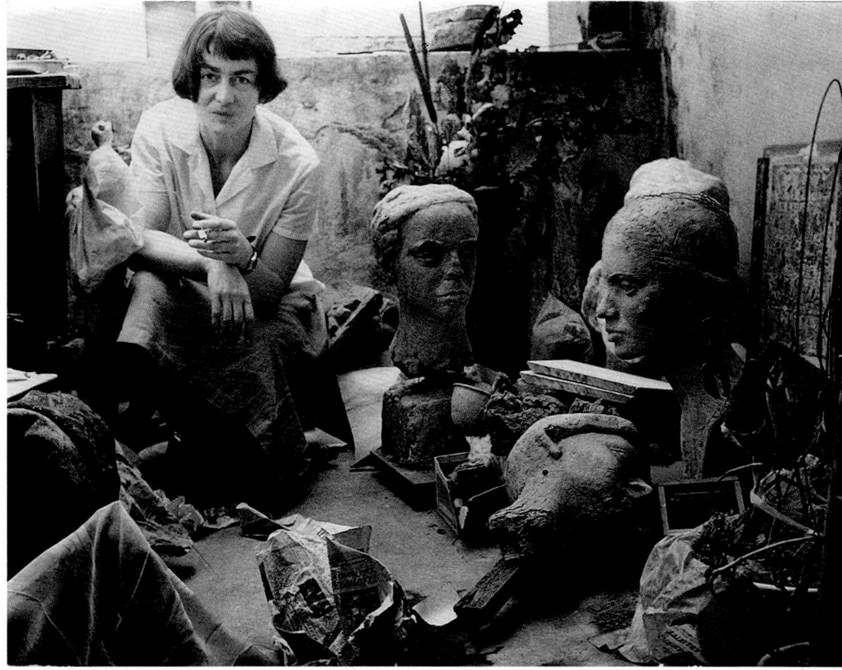

rather than political events or figureheads of the victorious new social order, accordingly comprised the major part of Jevrić's early sculptural output, and they were always motivated by her feelings and experiences – never by commissions. Thus both in terms of their form and spiritual significance, Jevrić's *Proposals* stood apart from the standard celebratory monumental (hyper)production of that era.

For her solo exhibition at ULUS Gallery in October 1957, Jevrić chose the title *Spatial Compositions*, aiming to emphasise the symbiosis of sculptural (spatial) and musical (compositional) elements in her work. The poet Vasko Popa contributed a preface to the modest

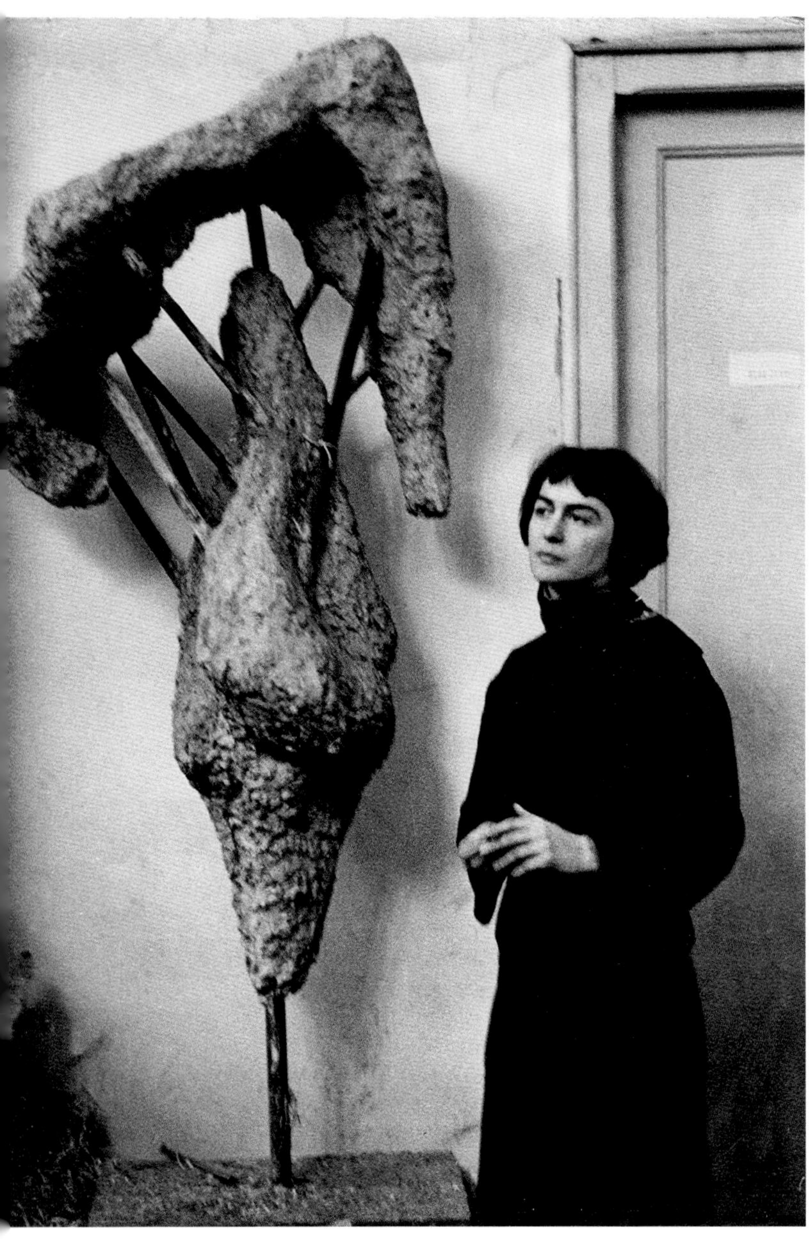

Olga Jevrić in her studio, Staro sajmište, Belgrade, 1959

catalogue for this exhibition. Art critics at the time generally praised this early entry onto the artistic stage,[4] but the two most insightful reviews came from authors outside the narrow professional art circles: the musicologist Pavle Stefanović and man of letters Jovan Hristić.[5] The success of the exhibition led to Jevrić being selected to participate in the Venice Biennale the next year. The artists who showed in the Yugoslav pavilion were chosen by Aleksa Čelebonović and included three prominent painters – Krsto Hegedušić, Gabrijel Stupica and Edo Murtić – as well as the sculptor Drago Tršar. Jevrić's biennale installation included two *Compositions* from 1956–57, three *Proposals for Monuments* (1957) and several works in smaller formats. Despite this modest selection coupled with the fact that the works were not well displayed, feedback from international art audiences[6] suggested that the display of her work represented a rare and timely inclusion of a Yugoslav artist in the wider contemporary context.[7] This contributed to the swift international recognition that followed.

Jevrić's critical success in both the domestic and international contexts stemmed from the markedly innovative conceptual and morpho-logical properties of her sculptural language. The first step in its development was the already mentioned *Proposal for a Monument* (Milanovac) of 1954, for which the artist took the traditional compact, closed *stećak* tombstone form and opened it up, incorporating free spatial voids between the vertical axes of the form. A crucial transformation occurred, however, with the drastic shift in her use of materials: instead of the gypsum and bronze casting of works such as the *Memento* series (1956–57), she began to

Olga Jevrić, Kikinda, Serbia, 1991

use sprayed iron and cement, and in the fourth
variant of the series introduced a metal rod
to hold together the separated and mutually
offset volumes. Numerous versions of her
Proposals for Monuments (1956–57) were based
precisely on this formal procedure, including
whole groups of sculptures to which the artist
attached specific titles, such as *Articulation
of Space*, *Complementary Forms* and *Concave
Complementary Forms*, *Three Elements* and
Vertical Composition. These titles suggest an
essentially abstract reflection on sculpture, one
that distanced itself from the employment of
anthropomorphic and organic forms. At the
time, even relatively innovative sculptors, either
directly or indirectly taking up the influence of
the (then almost unavoidable) role models of
Constantin Brâncuși, Jean Arp and Henry Moore,
commonly worked with reduced forms based on
the motif of the torso or the human figure. Jevrić
was thus significant in her complete bypassing
of these influences, instead developing her own
autonomous and non-referential sculptural
language. And it was this language, based on the
coordination of three basic elements – volumes,
rods and the space around and between them –
and accompanied by expressive suggestiveness
and symbolic connotations, that would launch
Olga Jevrić to the forefront of the national, and
soon afterwards international, art scene.

Jevrić's exhibition at the 1958 Venice Biennale
and the response to it from European art critics
raised the question of the typological classification of her sculptures. The French critic Pierre
Guéguen in his text *Sculpture d'aujourd'hui* made
mention of her work alongside that of Étienne
Martin, Alicia Penalba, Francesco Somaini,

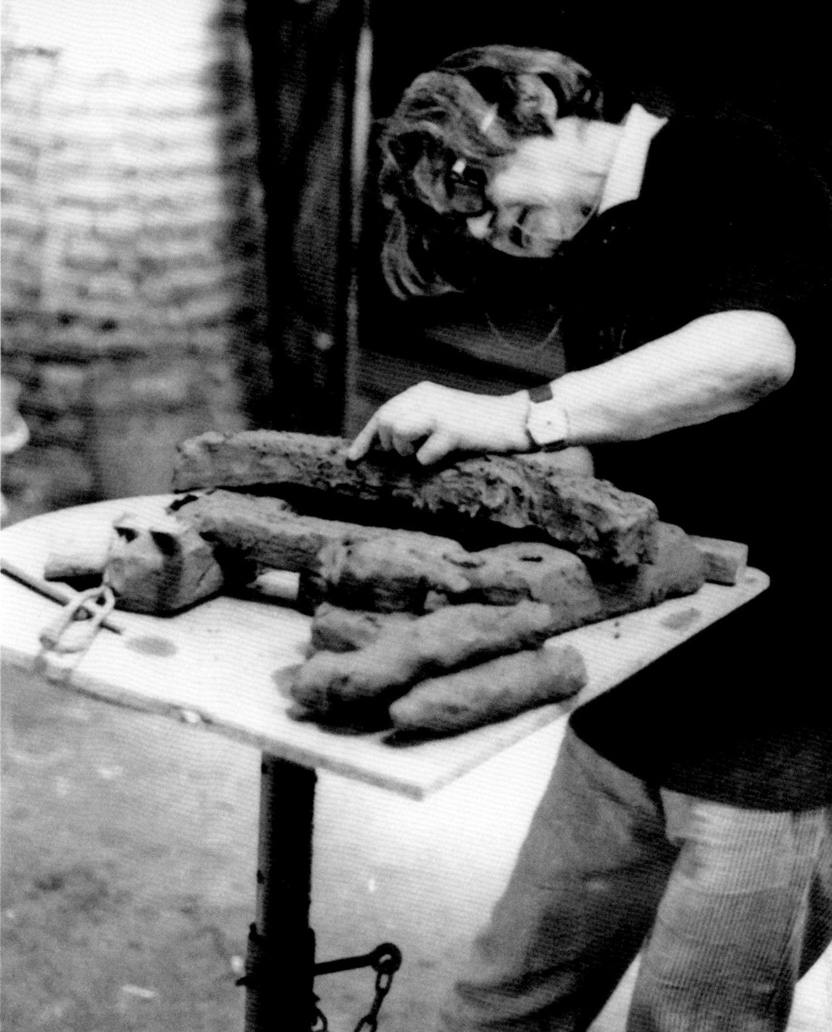

Charles Delahaye and Stanislas Wostan;[8] while
Luciano Pistoi of Notizie Gallery listed her alongside Eduardo Chillida, César, David Smith, Franco
Garelli and Claire Falkenstein as well as Somaini,
Martin and Delahaye.[9] Pistoi thus put forward the
claim that her sculpture shared proximity with
not only the formal but, above all, the spiritual
features of *art informel*. The artist herself,
however, was not inclined to this comparison
and, contrary to it, would insist on the essential
importance in her work of strict structural process
and construction. As she explained:

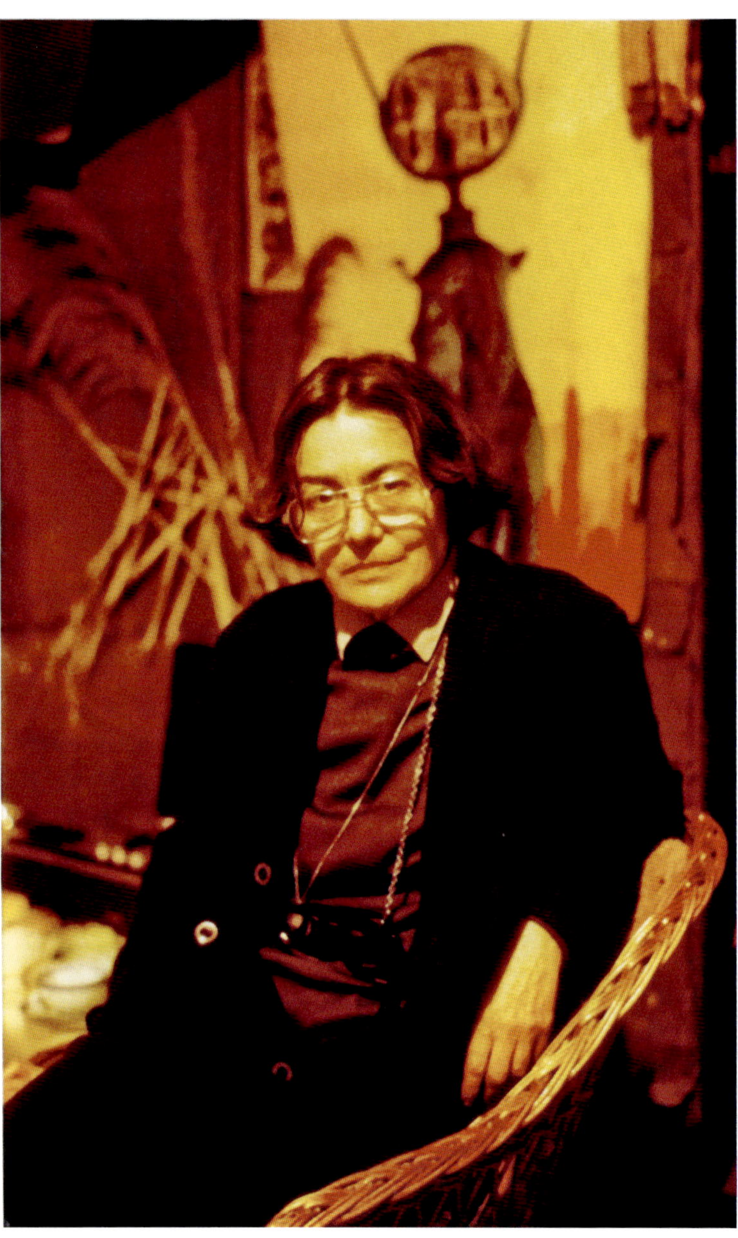

*I did not accept the classification of my work
as art informel, although this would imply
a considerably higher level of revolutionary
breakthrough in the realm of sculpture. My
sculpture is a composite unit emphatically
structured in space.*[10]

In line with this statement, the artist developed a unique formal working process, starting from preparatory studies and moving to preliminary designs in small formats, their modification into medium-sized works for the gallery and, finally – and quite rarely, because of the difficulty of realising the works – large outdoor scales. But each of these sculptures, regardless of the format, was an independent sculptural piece, thought out and consequently developed from the initial to the final stage. The artist was always fully aware of the reasons for and the effects of each formal intervention:

*My method of construction is based on
composite units composed of mass, space,
and lines of force, including the iron rods which
allow for motion in the formal sense (always
in conjunction with the assumed meaning) by
shifting the focus to the effects of space, and
by elaborating its problems as a medium, or
exploiting the infinite possibilities of informing
the volumes, their effects and mutual
relations, or by emphasising the role of the
iron rod which in the course of its movements
and in a mutual accord of directions and
measures allows for reviving the solutions and
maintaining them in their cause, for sustaining
them within the frameworks of the conceived
specific subjective universe.*[11]

Jevrić did not feel compelled to pursue international success by leaving her place of origin, and she was not at all attracted to entering the commercial gallery system. Staying in Belgrade, and despite her modest living conditions, she secured continuous work and took part in occasional and selective exhibitions, which she saw as a public check of her accomplished results. Thus, within a short period of time, she prepared two acclaimed solo shows: a concise retrospective at the Museum of Contemporary Art in Zagreb in February 1964, and an exhibition at the Salon of the Museum of Contemporary Art in Belgrade in October 1965, where she presented new works that had not yet been shown elsewhere. Though building on the firm conceptual foundations she had established earlier, these new works displayed significant changes in the treatment of certain basic elements of the artist's sculptural vocabulary. The volumes were now condensed and mutually closer, the rod was no longer primarily a support (and was occasionally even altogether absent from the composition), and the outer textures had become markedly expressive. These changes were also reflected in the titles of the sculptures and sculpture cycles: *Encompassed Space* (1964), *Convergent Massifs* (1965) and *Centripetal Forms* (1965), for example. As before, Jevrić put special emphasis on the capacity of each form to offer equally engaging and non-discriminate angles of observation: her sculpture never has a face and reverse but demands from the viewer a careful examination of each detail, requiring circulation around the three-dimensional body of the sculpture. Accordingly, the artist insisted that works be displayed at what she saw as the correct height and with carefully judged lighting. All these forms were small in size – 'the scale of my palm',[12] she would once say – but this did not take anything away from their plastic, expressive and symbolic effects, which remained essentially the same, regardless of the physical proportions in which the works were realised.

Although during the working process Jevrić tended to be preoccupied with thoroughly elaborating each formal detail, she occasionally pointed to the complex symbolic meanings of her sculptures in statements. In an interview to accompany her 1965 exhibition at the Museum of Contemporary Art, she said:

I strive to find a plastic metaphor able to communicate personally experienced truths and laws emerging from the causality of natural phenomena and the interrelations of human existence: the drama of conditionality, the concept of the subordination of the individual to the principle of universality, the unity of emergence and disappearance – reality in its contradictory essence.[13]

It thus becomes clear as to why the majority of her sculptures, even the small-scale studies, were intended to be developed into *Proposals for Monuments* (although she had to accept the impossibility of their realisation in the public sphere and at the desired scale). All her sculptures were, in essence, statements of spiritual dedication, to which the artist attached the following meanings:

Cataclysmic time – the time of collective tragedy and individual fate ripped up my generation's youth deeply; it lived in us as something unavoidable that could be communicated primarily as a memorial object, a symbol. This topic emerged as an inner urge, as a creative and ethical debt, as a need to leave a trace of particular consciousness about time and in time… True, none of them was realised, all of them remained in the scale of my palm… perhaps also because I did not wish to communicate such humane content in the form of banal, conventional standards, which would in turn revoke them. This present absurd time, plagued by frightening demonic forces, deprives me of the power of utterance as an artist.[14]

The refusal to 'communicate humane content' according to 'banal, conventional standards' in fact points to essential aspects of Jevrić's attitude to her artistic vocation and professional position, and, ultimately, to her fundamental ethical virtues. These include her total commitment to the artist's vocation; her acceptance of her ultimate responsibility for each single act undertaken publicly; and her awareness of belonging to the culture of her milieu and of the obligation to adapt to it with her own contributions, while at the same time, in the concrete social circumstances and under the existing political order, preserving, above all, her individual autonomy as an artist and as a human being. With such an attitude towards life, she withstood with dignity certain deprivations in the initial period of her artistic career, as well as the recognition she gained in the mature and late periods of her life. In an artistic milieu with a moderate heritage of modern sculpture, she demonstrated that it was possible to propose a new sculptural language, one that was quite radical and critically relevant not only locally but also internationally. Her success was founded on the manual execution of singular sculptures in accordance with the basic formal demands of this timeless discipline – rather than pursuing other sculptural tendencies that gained traction internationally in the years she matured as an artist (such as assemblage, the minimalist specific object, 'sculpture in the expanded field', installation and so on). Because of this her output appears even more significant – it is perhaps even unique in terms of its concepts and complexities. In both her work and her life Jevrić thus represents an exceptional figure of Serbian artistic culture in the crucial period of its urgent and accelerated modernisation.

NOTES

1 For more details see catalogue of the retrospective exhibition, Museum of Contemporary Art, Belgrade, 1981; catalogue of the retrospective exhibition, Gallery SANU, Belgrade, 2001; J. Denegri, *Olga Jevrić*, Topy and Vojnoizdavački zavod, Belgrade, 2005; catalogue of the retrospective exhibition, Heritage House, Belgrade, 2012.

2 Interview with Vesna Majher, *Kazivanja i iskazi srpskih vajara*, Belgrade, 2006.

3 Video interview with J. Denegri, German Cultural Centre, Belgrade, February 2001, reprinted in Denegri, *op. cit.*, p.83.

4 M. Kolarić, 'Prostorne kompozicije Olge Jevrić', *Večernje novosti*, 18 October 1957; P. Vasić, 'Traženja Olge Jevrić', *Politika*, 19 October 1957; Đ. Popović, 'Izložbe Olge Jevrić i Miće Nikolajevića', *Borba*, 22 October 1957; M. B. Protić, 'Izložba Olge Jevrić', *NIN*, 27 October 1957; R. Predić, 'Olga Jevrić', *Vidici*, no.32, 1957; R. Predić, 'Vajarstvo koje tek treba da stekne svoju legitimnost i priznanje', *Letopis Matice srpske*, December 1957.

5 P. Stefanović, 'Ispovest i poruke jednog savremenog vajara', *Umetnost* (Zagreb), vols.7–8, no.II, Zagreb 1958; J. Hristić, 'Olga Jevrić ili ontologija vajarskog dela', *Delo*, 2, February 1960.

6 C. Doelman, 'De Biennale', *Nieuwe Rotterdamse courant*, 5 July 1958; Ch. Delloye, 'La sculture à la Biennale', *Aujourd'hui*, no.19, 1958; G. Marchiori, 'La XXIX Biennale di Venezia', *Art International*, nos.6–7, 1958; J. Fitzsimmons, 'Space and Image in Art (à propos of the XXIX Biennale in Venice)', *Quadrum*, no.6, 1958; H. Wecher, 'Les participations Espagnole et Yugoslavie à la XXIX Biennale de Venise', *Quadrum*, no.6, 1958; H. Wecher, 'La Biennale de Venise', *Cimaise*, no.6, 1958; L. Pistoi, '11 appunti veneziani', *Notizie*, no.6, 1958; G. Dorfles, 'La scultura straniera alla Biennale', *Domus*, no.247, 1958; G. Dorfles, 'La macchia e il gesto alla 29. Biennale', *Aut-Aut*, 1958; E. Crispolti, 'Per uno bilancio della Biennale 1958', *Il taccuino delle arti*, no.32, 1958; A. Montanari, 'Vitale partecipazione della Jugoslavia all'evoluzione europea', *Il taccuino delle arti*, no.32, 1958; A. Jouffroy, 'La pavillon Yougoslave', *Arts*, no.675, 1958.

7 To give some context, other artists who exhibited at the Venice Biennale that year included Wols in the central pavilion; Mark Tobey, Mark Rothko, David Smith and Seymour Lipton in the US pavilion; William Scott and Stanley William Hayter in the British pavilion; Lucio Fontana and Alberto Burri in the Italian pavilion; André Masson in the French pavilion; Karl Otto Götz, Emil Schumacher and K.R.H. Sonderborg in the German pavilion; and a particularly strong selection of then young Spanish artists, including the painters Antoni Tàpies, Manolo Millares, Antonio Saura and Luis Feito, and with Eduardo Chillida as winner of the award for sculpture.

For the occasion of Jevrić's participation, Vera Horvat Pintarić contributed a text that was crucial for understanding the concerns of Jevrić's work in an international context. It was first published in the journal of the Notizie Gallery during the 1959 solo exhibition in Turin. V. Horvat Pintarić, 'O skulpturi Olge Jevrić', *Književnik*, no.14, 1960, reprinted in the book *Kritike i eseji*, HAZU, Zagreb, 2012.

8 P. Guéguen, 'Sculpture d'aujourd'hui', *Aujord'hui*, no.19, 1958.

9 L. Pistoi, 'Incontro con Olga Jevrić', *Notizie*, vol.10, 1959.

10 Interview with Marija Đorđević, *Politika*, 19 May 2001.

11 Interview with J. Denegri, February 2001, reprinted in Denegri, *op. cit.*

12 Interview with Dragana Špiljević, Radio Jugoslavija, 4 November 1991.

13 Interview with Dragoslav Adamović, 'Želim da u formu utisnem jedno ljudsko iskustvo', *Politika*, 14 November 1965.

14 Interview with Dragana Špiljević, *op. cit.*

Olga Jevrić

Sculpture

PEER, London
28 June–14 September 2019

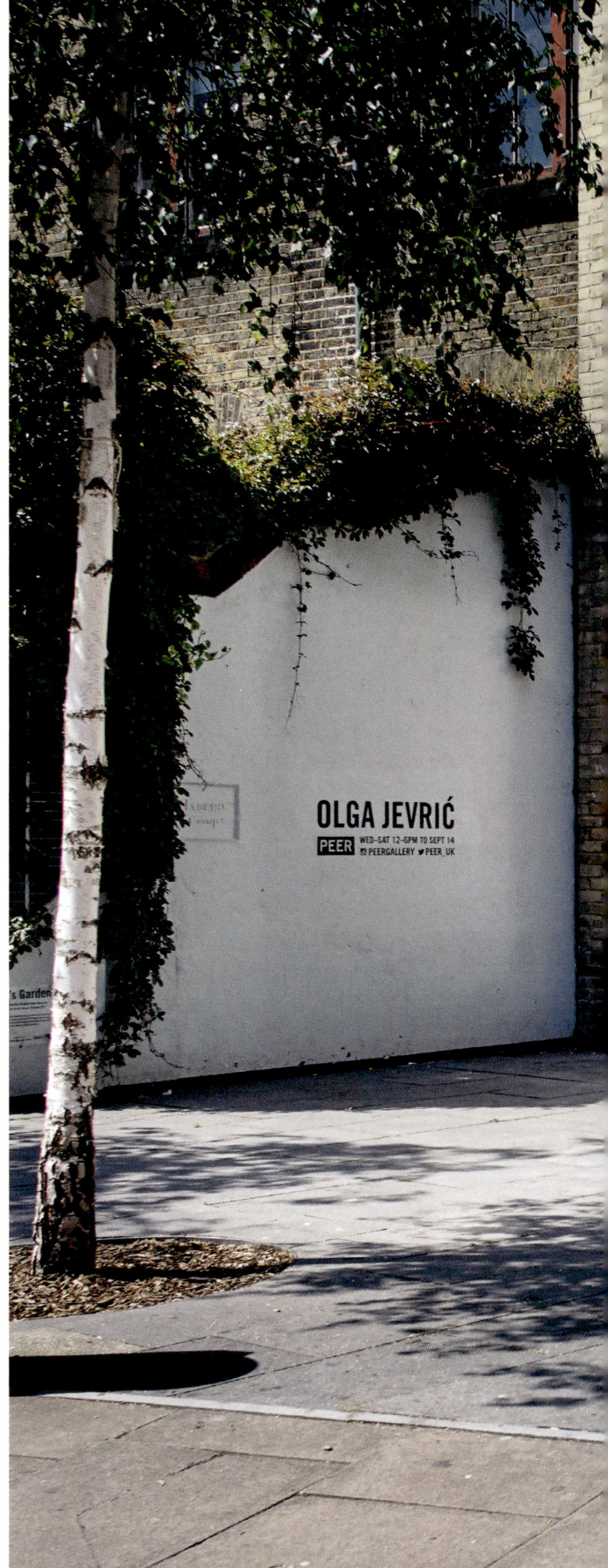

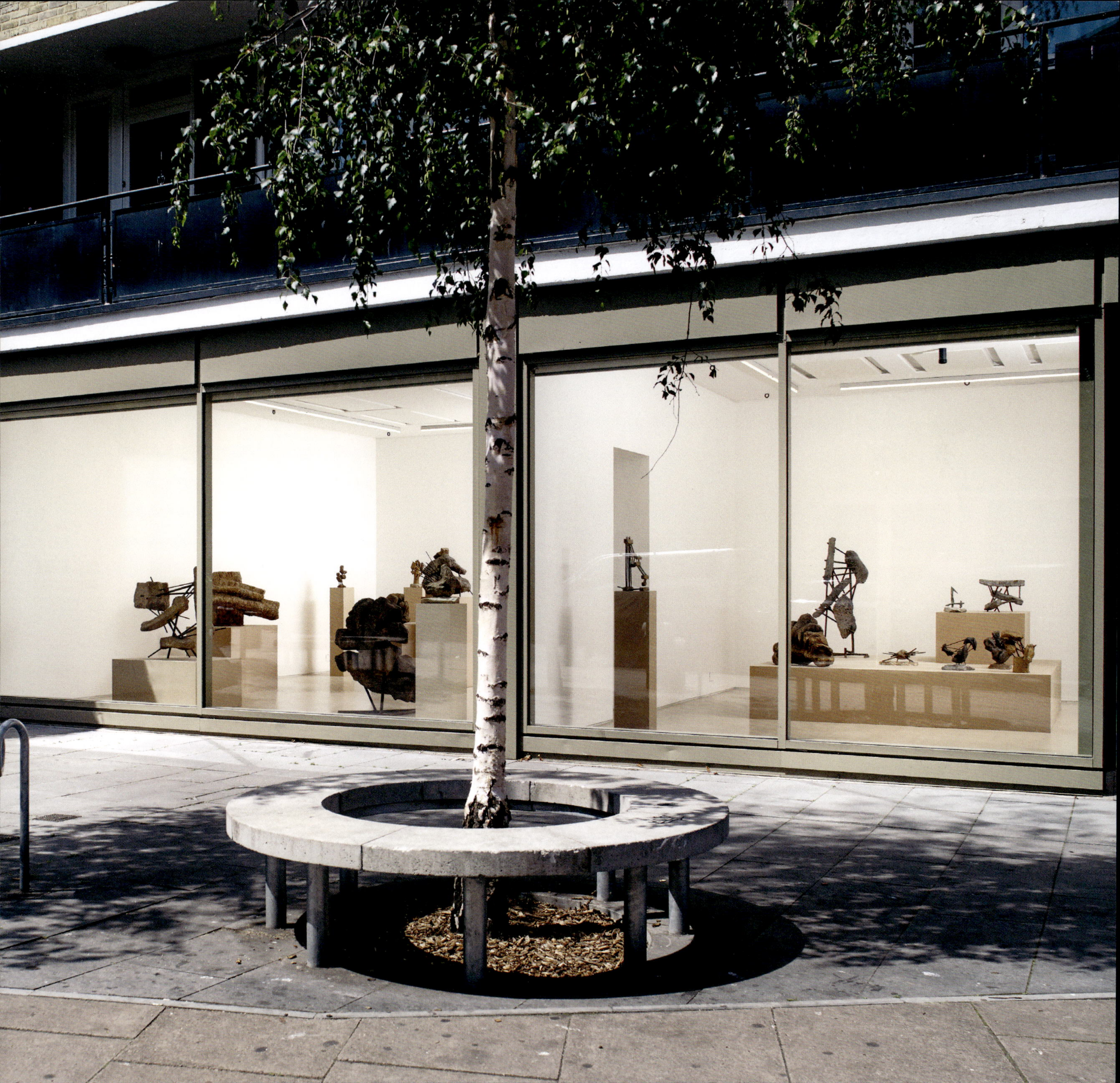

foreground

***Weaving through Space**, 1969/78*
Ferric oxide, iron, 41.5 × 18 × 21 cm
Serbian Academy of Sciences and Arts, Belgrade

background

***Small Intersection Ib**, 1985–2001*
Ferric oxide, 61 × 48 × 100 cm
Heritage House, Belgrade

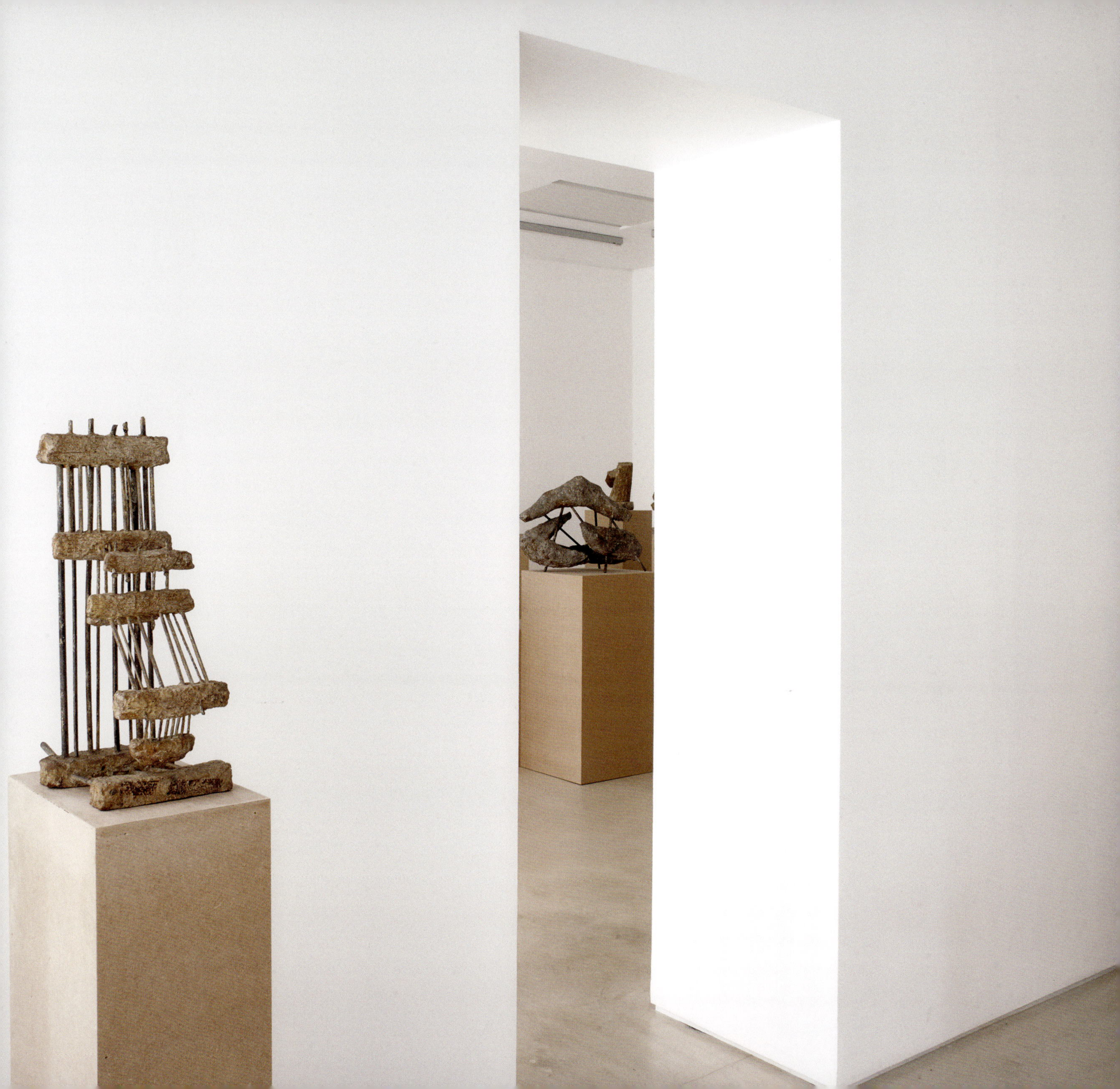

The Form in Origination 1a, 1964
Cement, 45 × 60 × 39 cm
Heritage House, Belgrade

Articulation of Space Ia, 1956
Cement, iron, 117 × 66 × 44 cm
Heritage House, Belgrade

Emination I, 1970–83
Ferric oxide, iron, 13 × 37 × 11 cm
Serbian Academy of Sciences and
Arts, Belgrade

Constellation, 1959
Sprayed iron, 27 × 28 × 29 cm
Serbian Academy of Sciences and
Arts, Belgrade

Centripetal Form I, 1964–5
Ferric oxide, iron, 28 × 24.5 × 15 cm
Serbian Academy of Sciences and
Arts, Belgrade

Astatic Composition IIa, 1969–75
Ferric oxide, iron, 33.5 × 25 × 23 cm
Heritage House, Belgrade

raised plinth, left to right

Memento I, 1956 (cast in 1982)
Bronze, 23 × 17 × 8.5 cm
Museum of Contemporary Art,
Belgrade

Articulation of Space II, 1956–7
Cement, iron, 29 × 45 × 32 cm
Heritage House, Belgrade

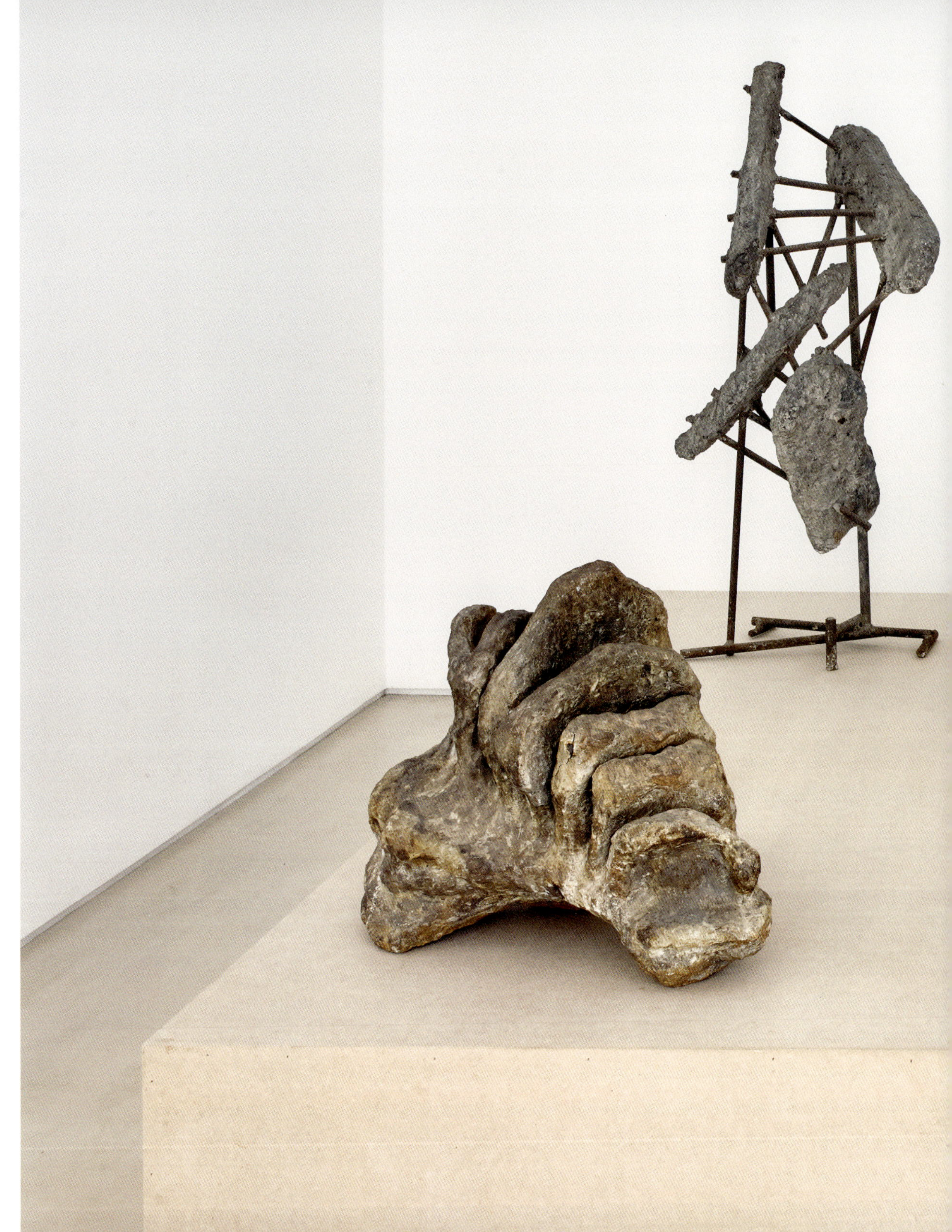

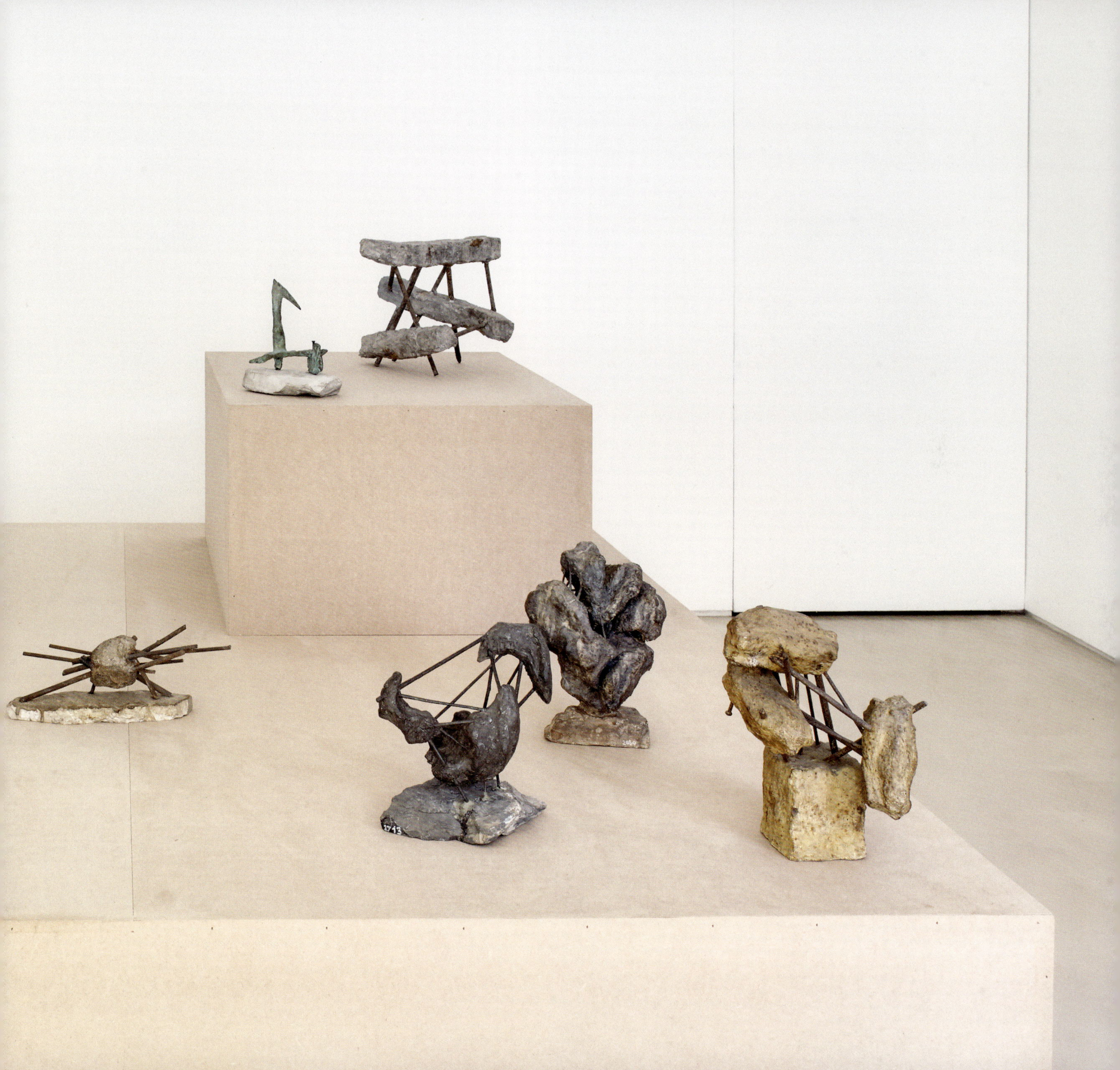

background

Small Intersection Ib, 1985-2001
Ferric oxide, 61 × 48 × 100 cm
Heritage House, Belgrade

foreground, clockwise from top right plinth

Memento I, 1956 (cast in 1982)
Bronze, 23 × 17 × 8.5 cm
Museum of Contemporary Art, Belgrade

Centripetal Form I, 1964-5
Ferric oxide, iron, 28 × 24.5 × 15 cm
Serbian Academy of Sciences and Arts,
Belgrade

Astatic Composition IIa, 1969-75
Ferric oxide, iron, 33.5 × 25 × 23 cm
Heritage House, Belgrade

Constellation, 1959
Sprayed iron, 27 x 28 x 29 cm
Serbian Academy of Sciences and Arts,
Belgrade

Emination I, 1970-83
Ferric oxide, iron, 13 × 37 × 11 cm
Serbian Academy of Sciences and Arts,
Belgrade

The Form in Origination 1a, 1964
Cement, 45 × 60 × 39 cm
Heritage House, Belgrade

Articulation of Space Ia, 1956
Cement, iron, 117 × 66 × 44 cm
Heritage House, Belgrade

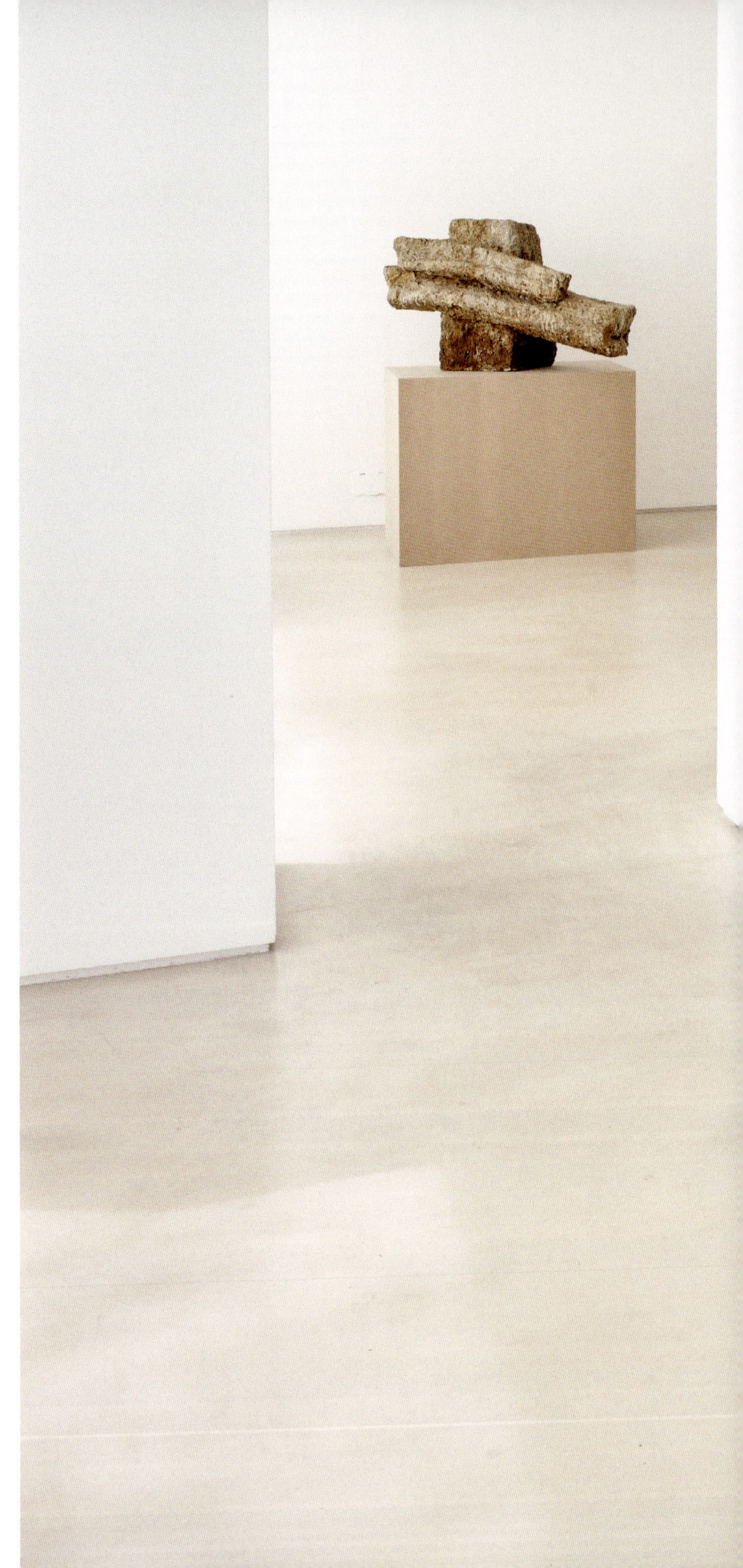

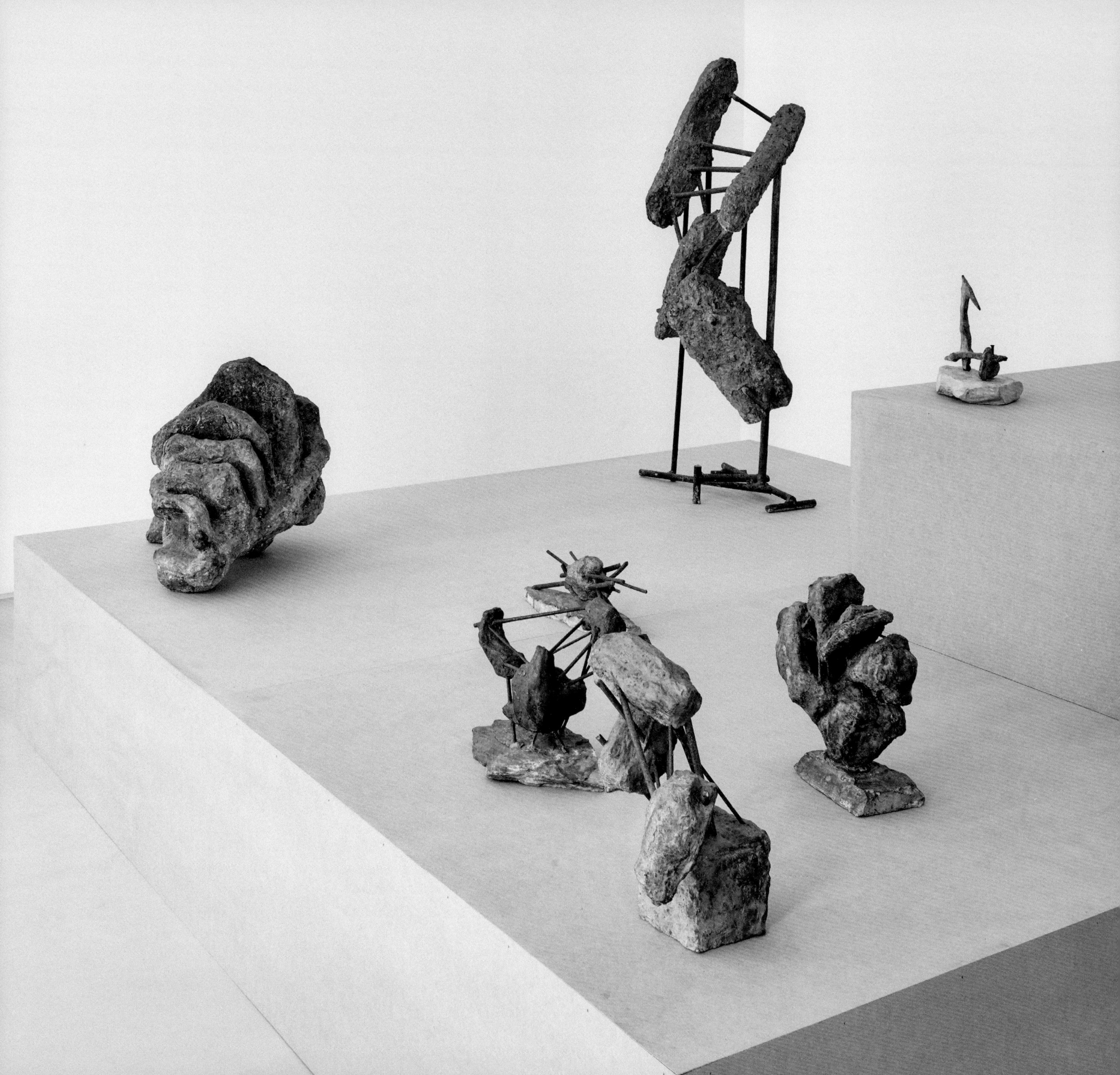

Reverse view of the installation shown
on the previous spread

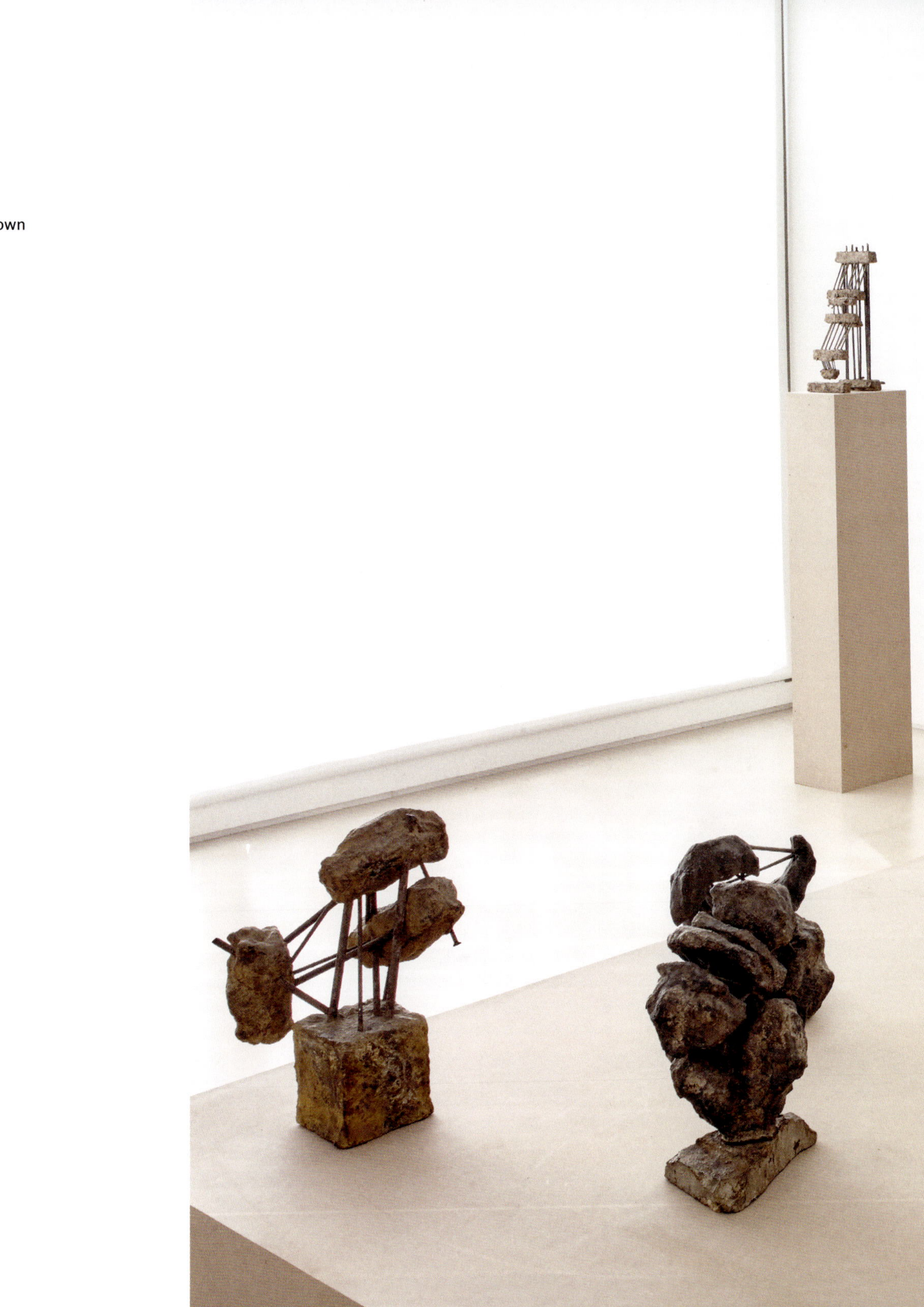

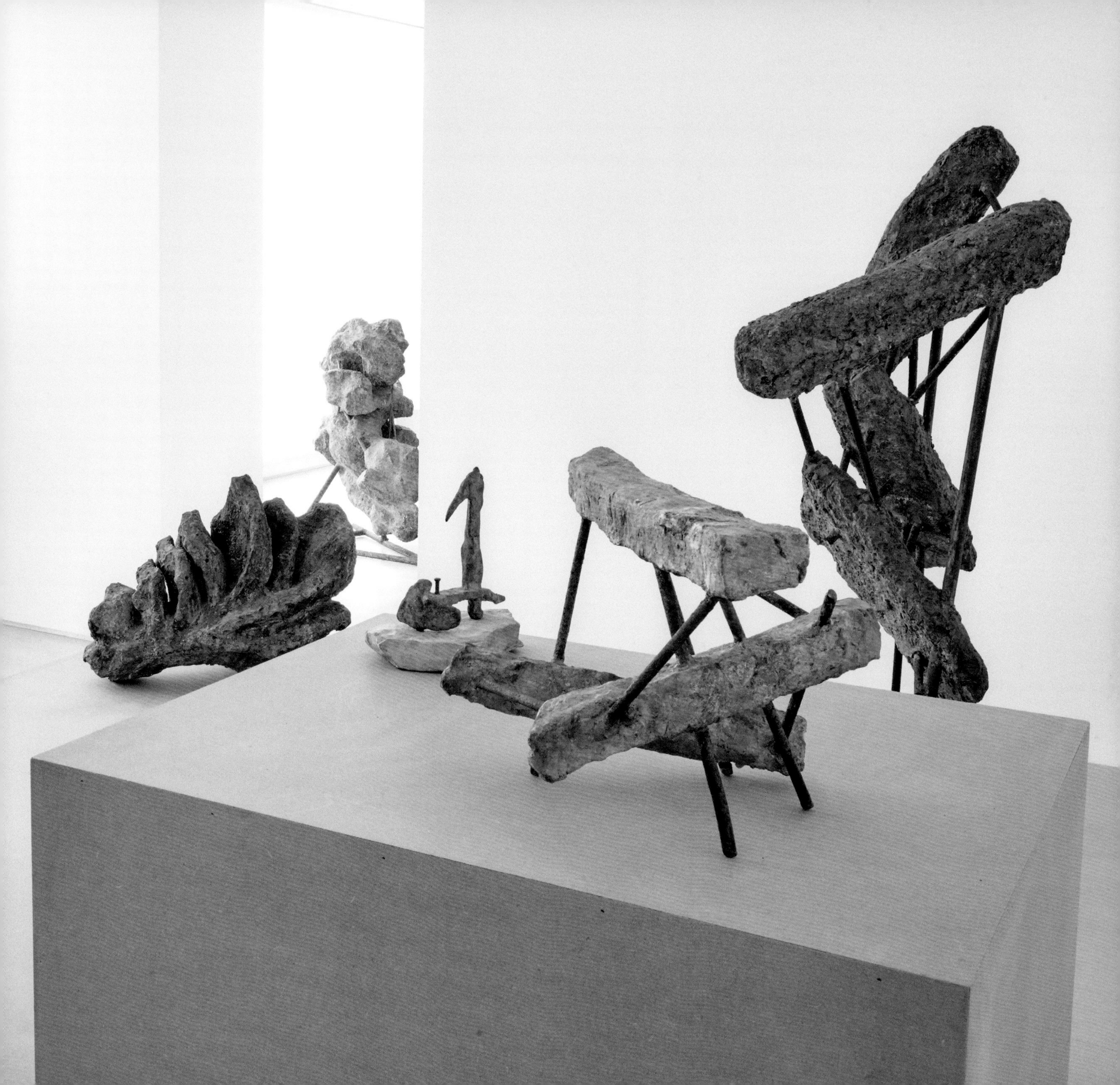

left to right

Dichotomous Shape, 1966–68
Ferric oxide, iron, 103 × 104 × 64 cm
Heritage House, Belgrade

Articulation of Space VIII, 1970–81
Ferric oxide, iron, 89.5 × 100 × 82 cm
Serbian Academy of Sciences and Arts, Belgrade

Small Intersection Ib, 1985–2001
Ferric oxide, 61 × 48 × 100 cm
Heritage House, Belgrade

following pages

General view of the installation at PEER

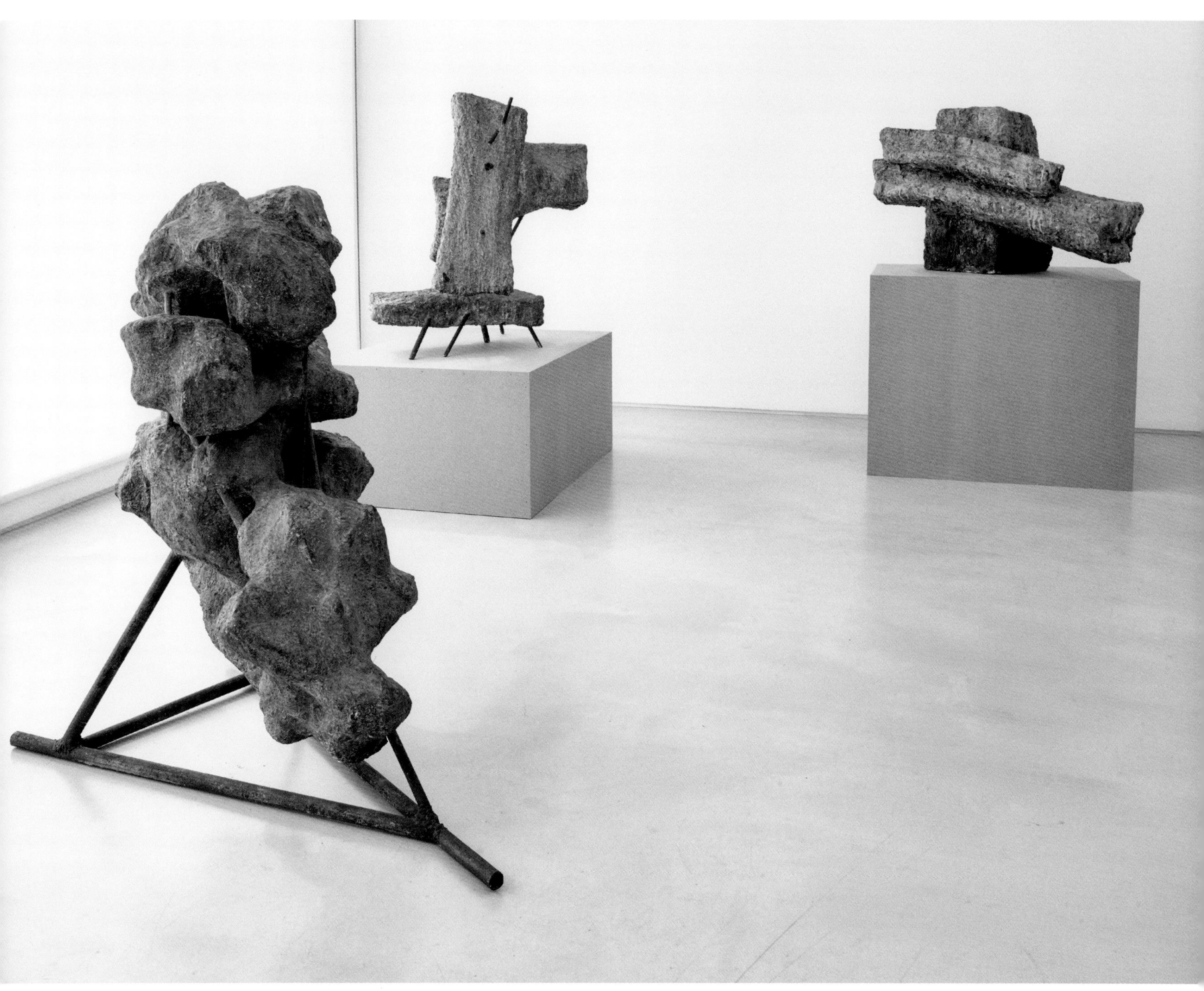

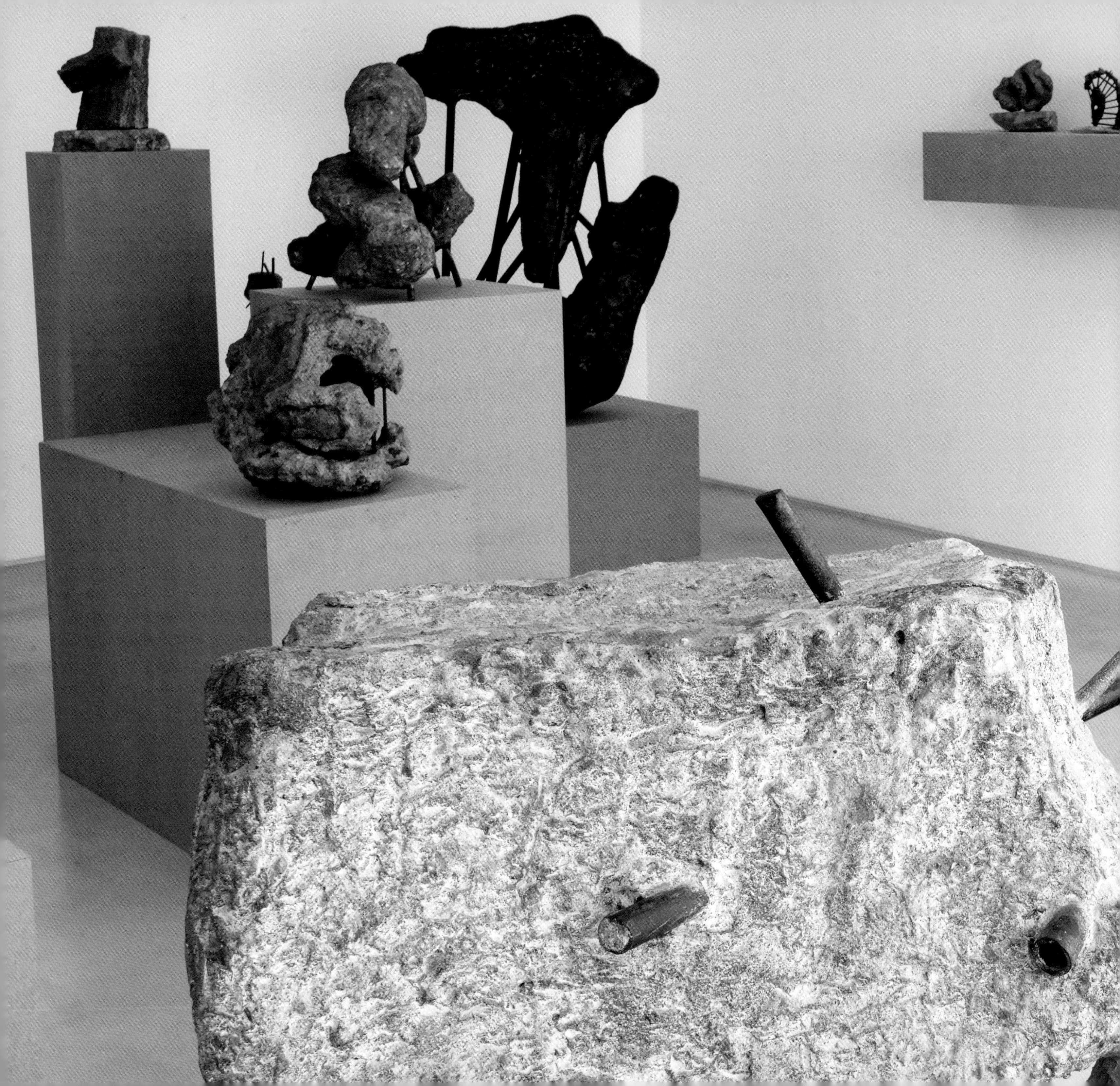

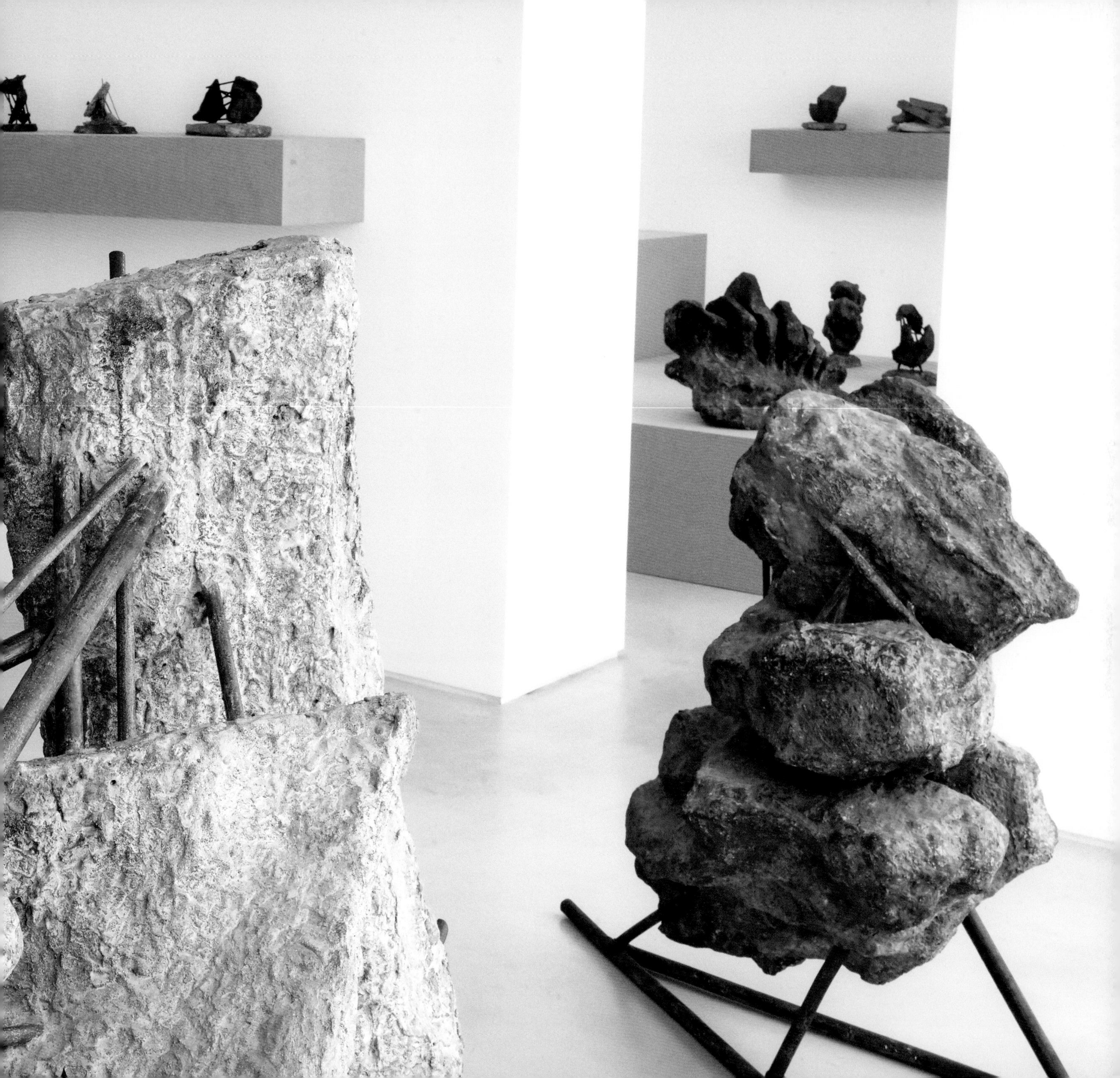

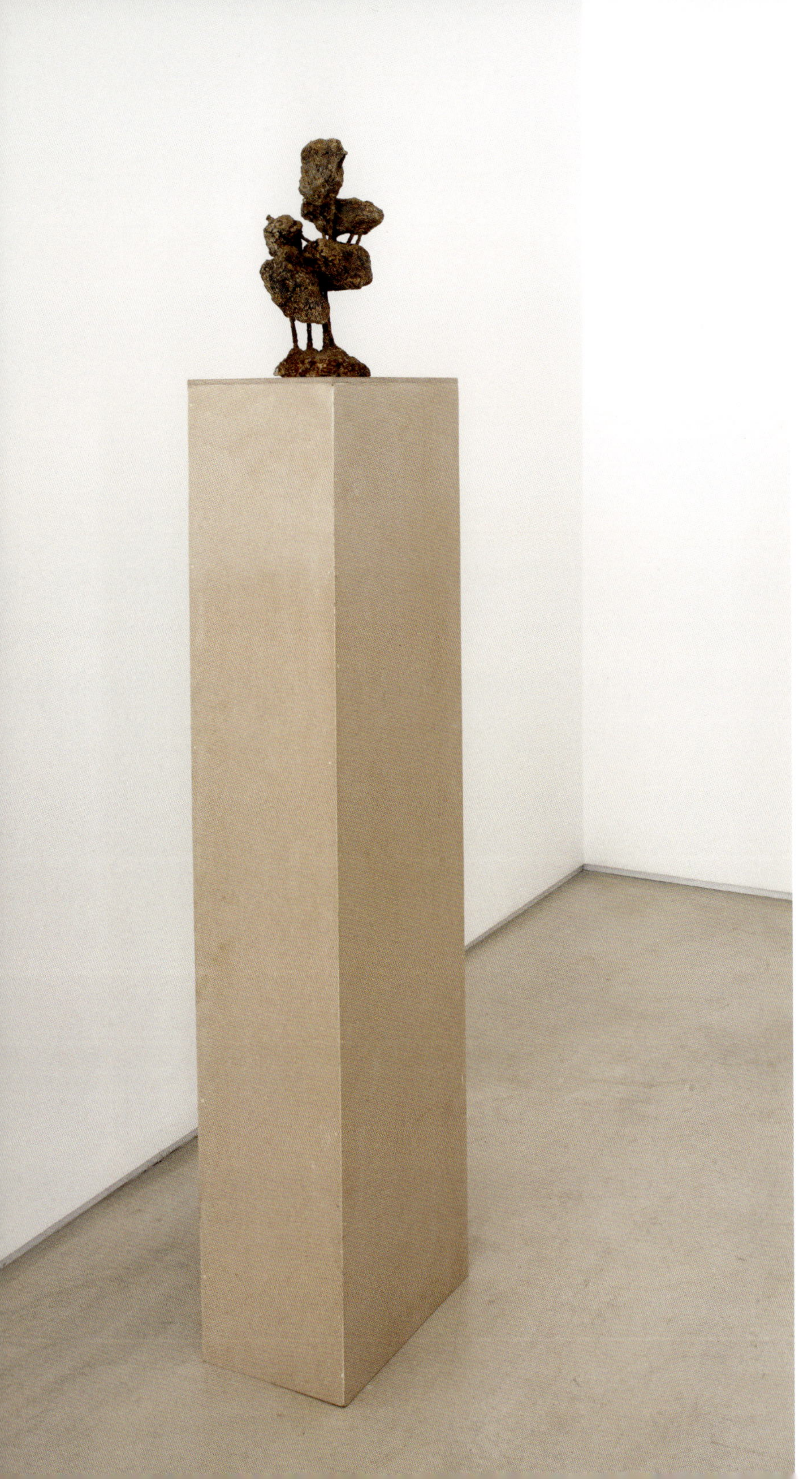

left

Five Massifs, 1965
Ferric oxide, iron, 24.5 × 16 × 9 cm
Serbian Academy of Sciences and Arts,
Belgrade

opposite, from left to right

Permeation 1, 1986
Ferric oxide, 22.5 × 17 × 15.5 cm
Serbian Academy of Sciences and Arts,
Belgrade

Two Member Set – Exostructure, 1972–7
Ferric oxide, iron, 31 × 18.5 × 16 cm
Serbian Academy of Sciences and Arts,
Belgrade

Axial Configuration, 1969–71
Ferric oxide, iron, 32 × 17 × 18 cm
Serbian Academy of Sciences and Arts,
Belgrade

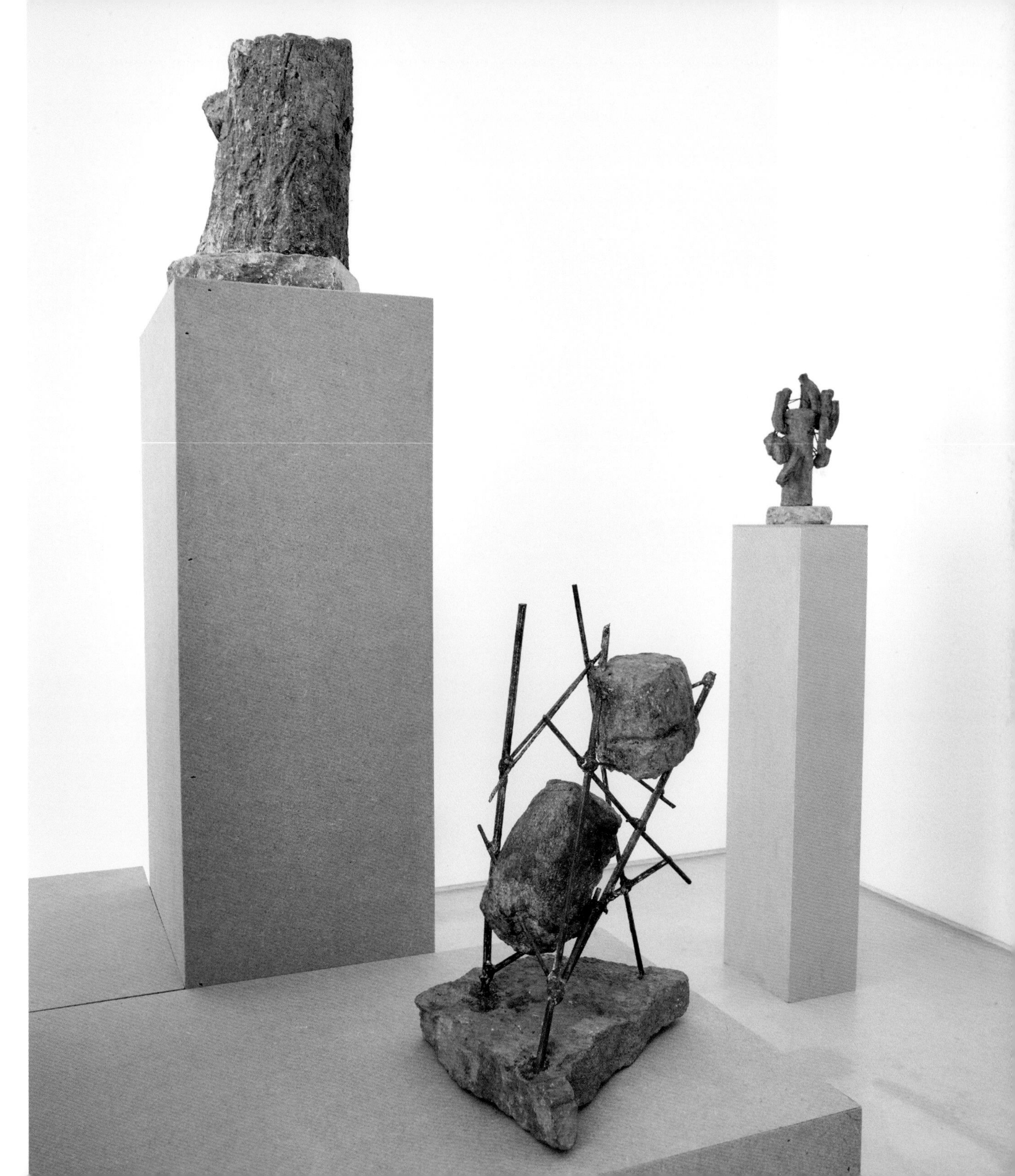

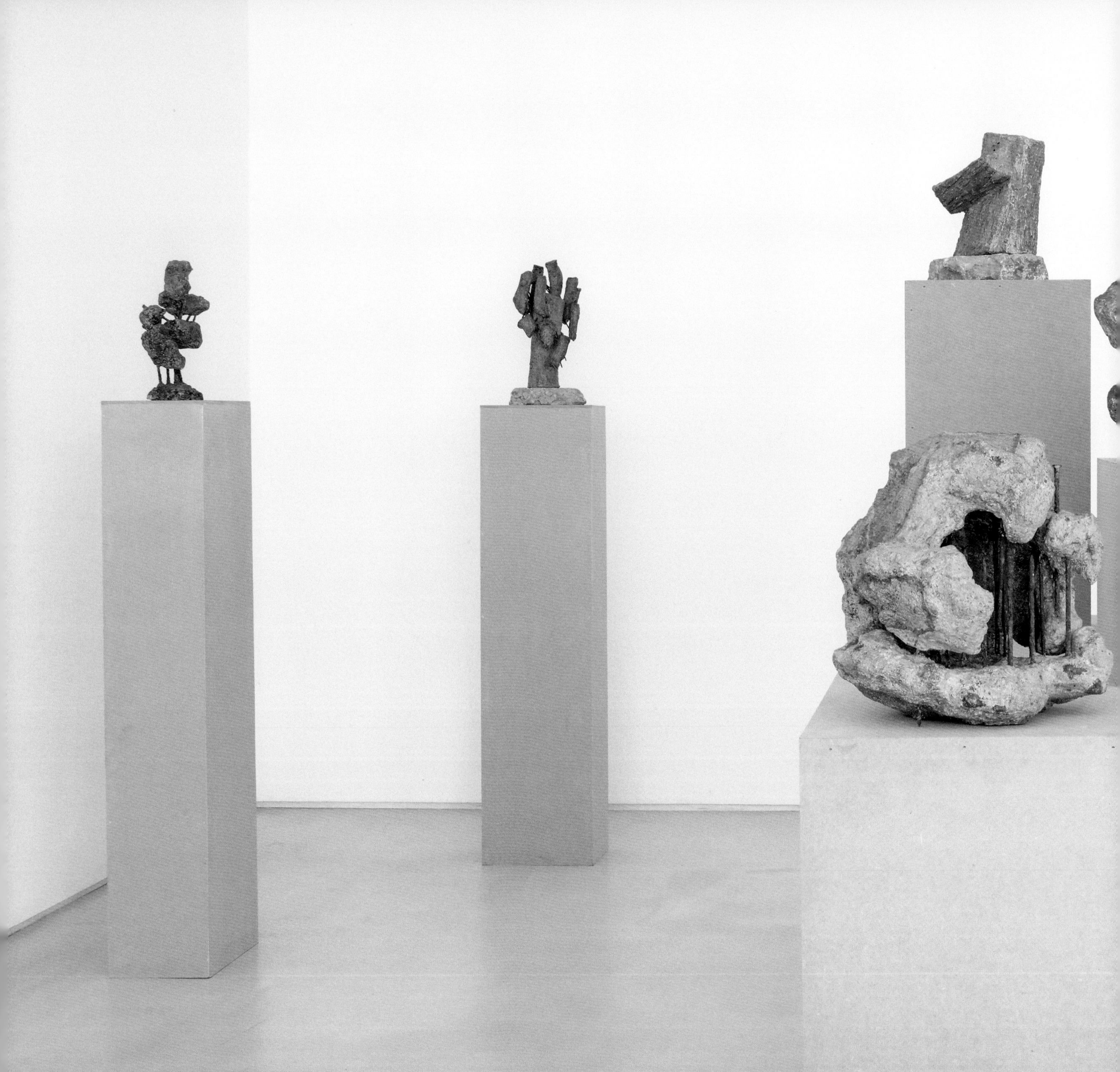

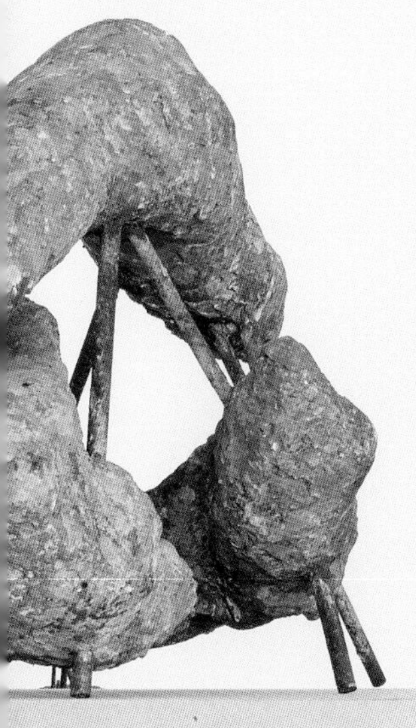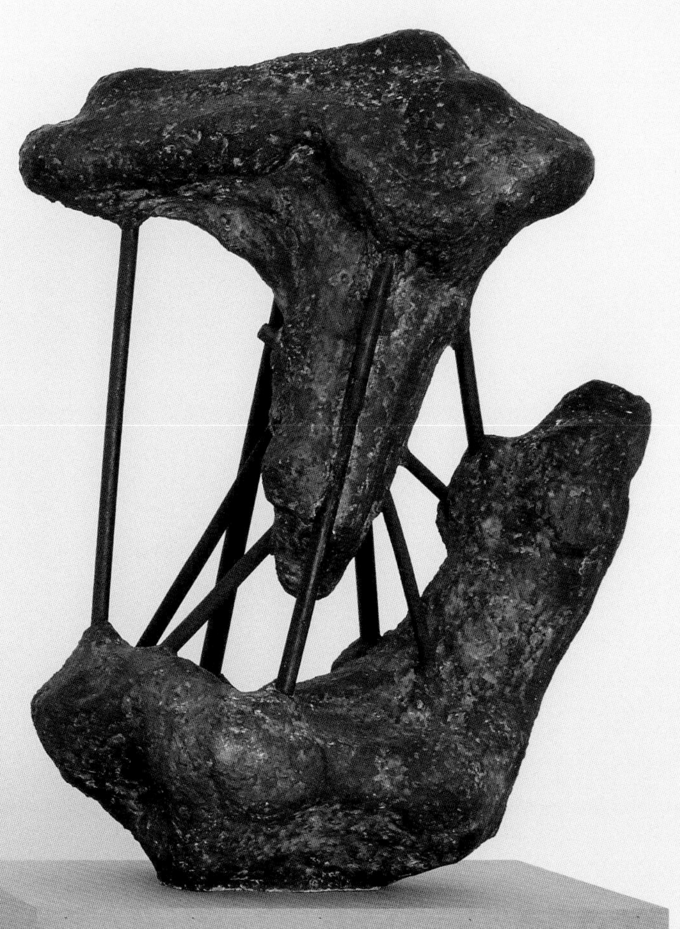

left to right

Five Massifs, 1965
Ferric oxide, iron, 24.5 x 16 x 9 cm
Serbian Academy of Sciences and
Arts, Belgrade

Axial Configuration, 1969–71
Ferric oxide, iron , 32 × 17 × 18 cm
Serbian Academy of Sciences and
Arts, Belgrade

Space in a Habitat, 1966–74
Ferric oxide, iron, 37 × 40 × 78 cm
Heritage House, Belgrade

Permeation 1, 1986
Ferric oxide, 22.5 × 17 × 15.5 cm
Serbian Academy of Sciences and
Arts, Belgrade

Three Elements Ia, 1955–6
Cement, iron, 14 × 12 × 13 cm
Heritage House, Belgrade

Complementary Forms, 1956–7
Bronze, 121.4 × 89 × 52 cm
Museum of Contemporary Art,
Belgrade

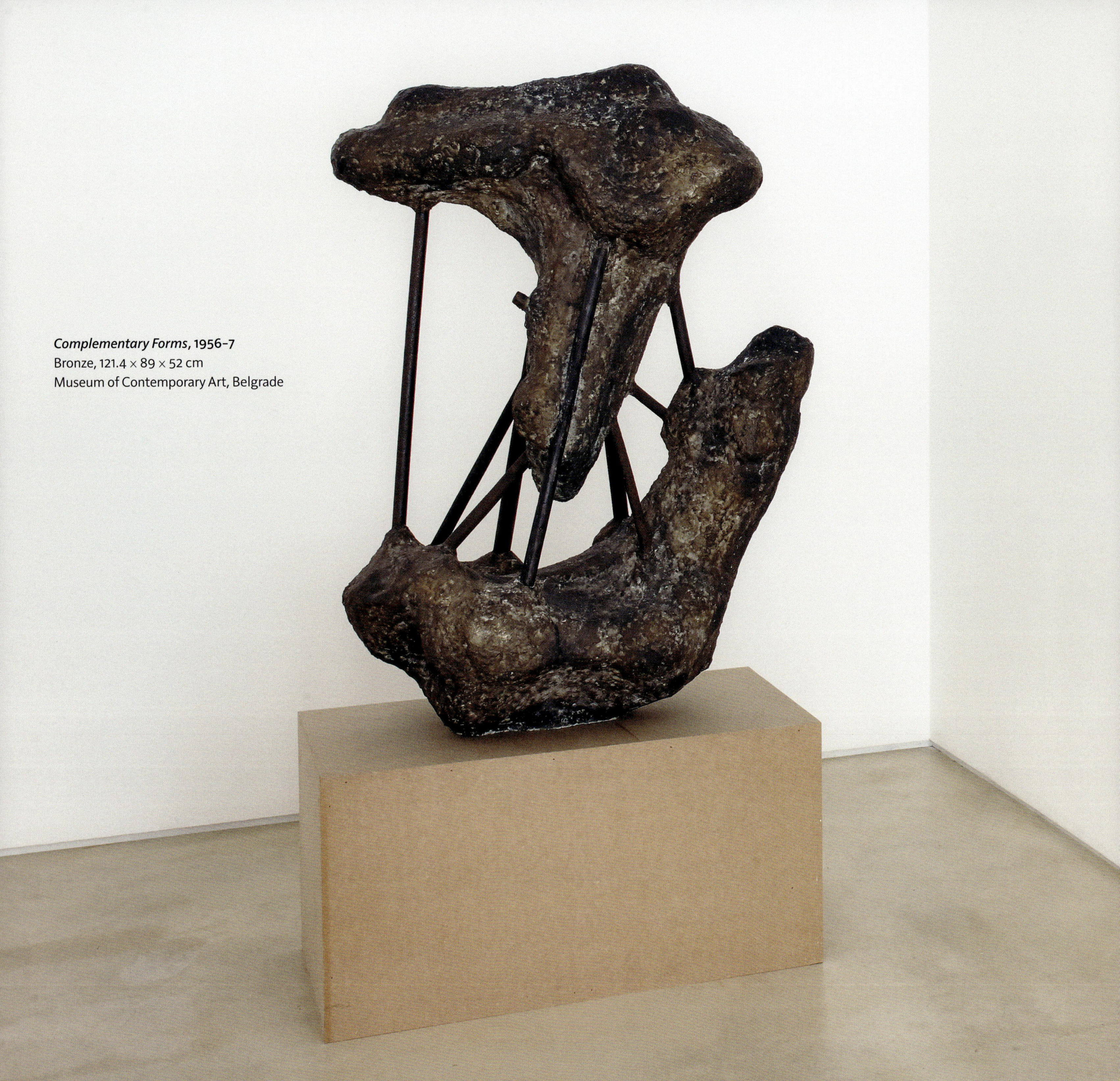

Complementary Forms, 1956–7
Bronze, 121.4 × 89 × 52 cm
Museum of Contemporary Art, Belgrade

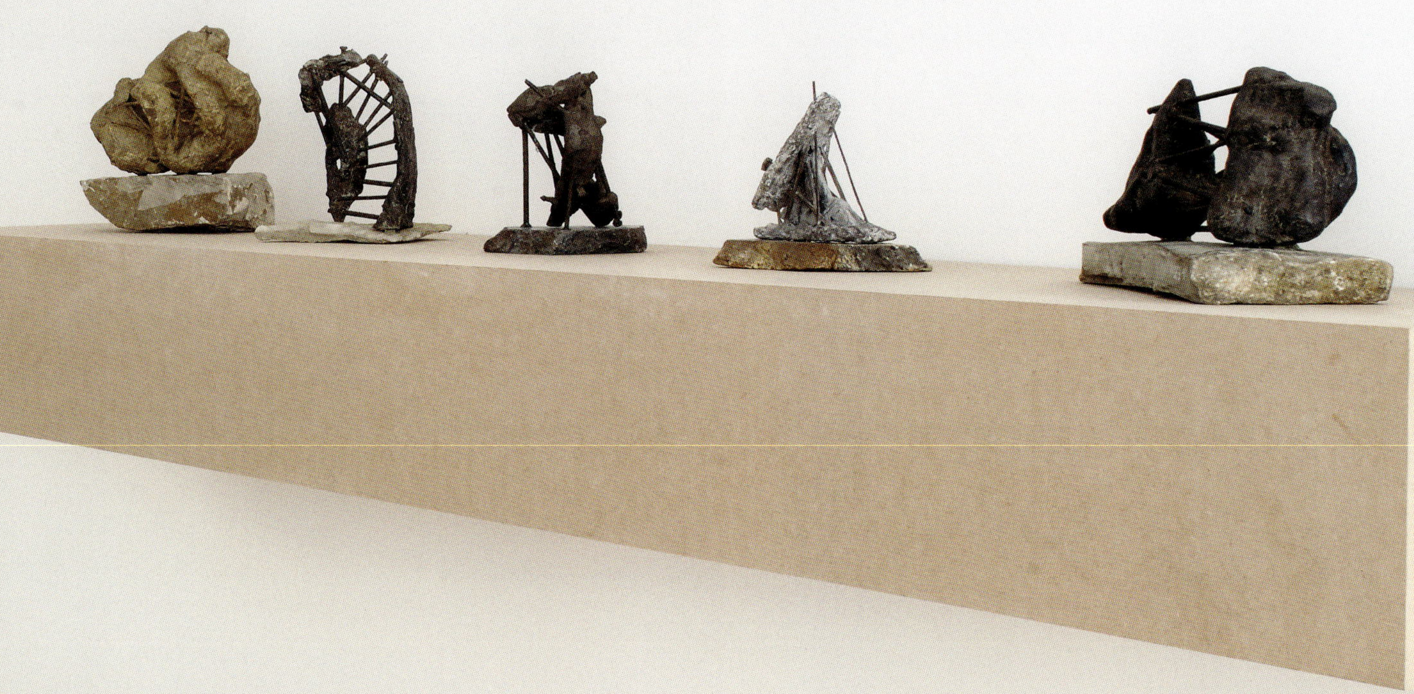

above, left to right

Cavernous Shape I, 1965
Ferric oxide, iron, 14 × 17.5 × 12.5 cm

Shielded Shape I (Harp), 1956
Sprayed iron, 17 × 13.5 × 10 cm

Three Elements III, 1956
Ferric oxide, iron, 14 × 12 × 13 cm

Proposal for a Monument, Zev, 1958
Ferric oxide, iron, 11.5 × 13 × 7 cm

Aggressive Forms I, 1959
Sprayed iron, 12 × 25.5 × 8.5 cm

All Serbian Academy of Sciences
and Arts, Belgrade

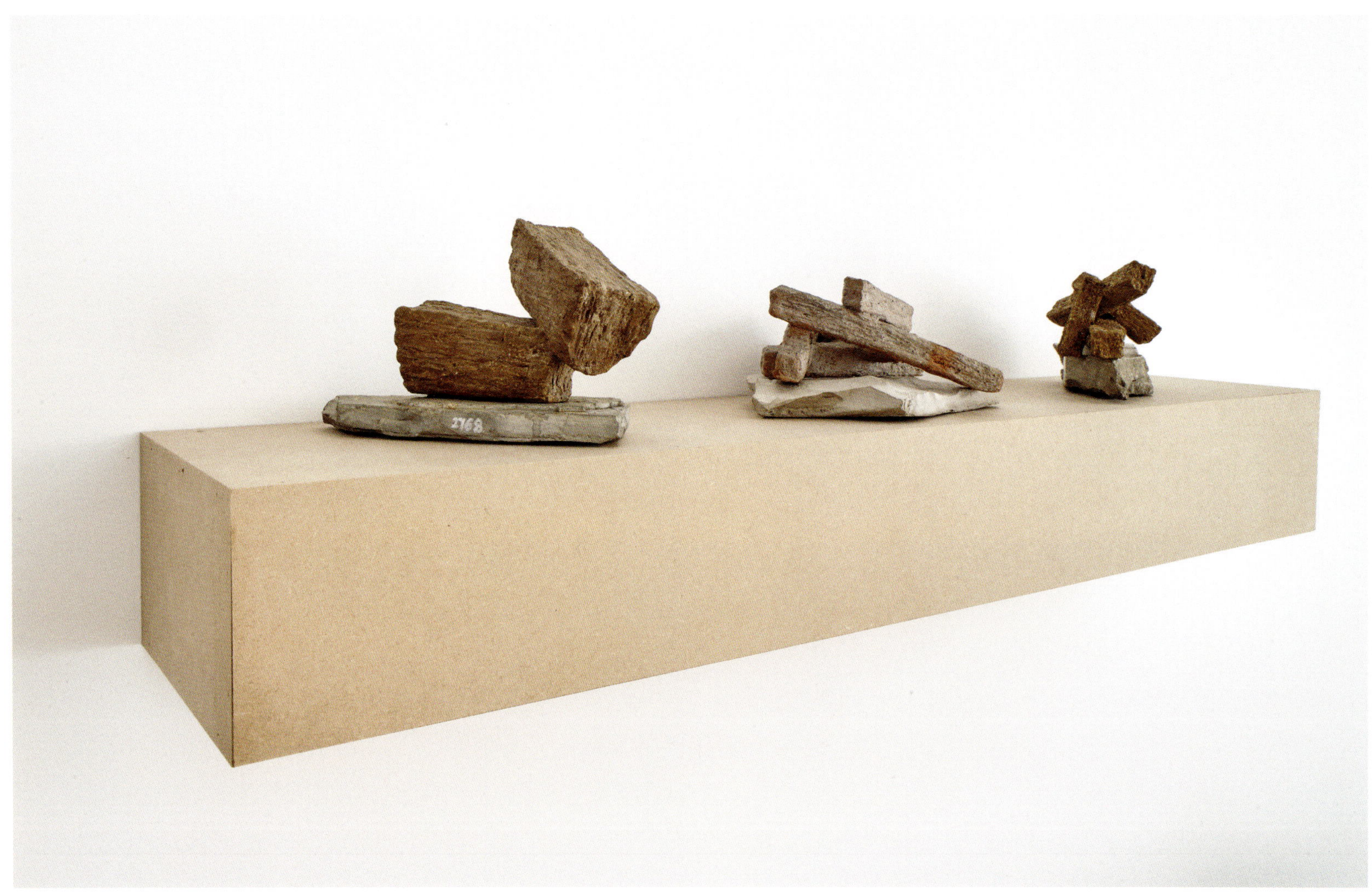

above, left to right

Astatic Relation II, 1990
Ferric oxide, 17 × 25 × 18 cm

Interweaving, 1993
Terracotta, 12 × 26.5 × 28 cm

Gredna II, 1996
Ferric oxide, 14 × 33 × 17 cm

All Serbian Academy of Sciences
and Arts, Belgrade

Hiatus Ia, 1967–73
Ferric oxide, iron, 36 × 34.5 × 17.5 cm
Serbian Academy of Sciences
and Arts, Belgrade

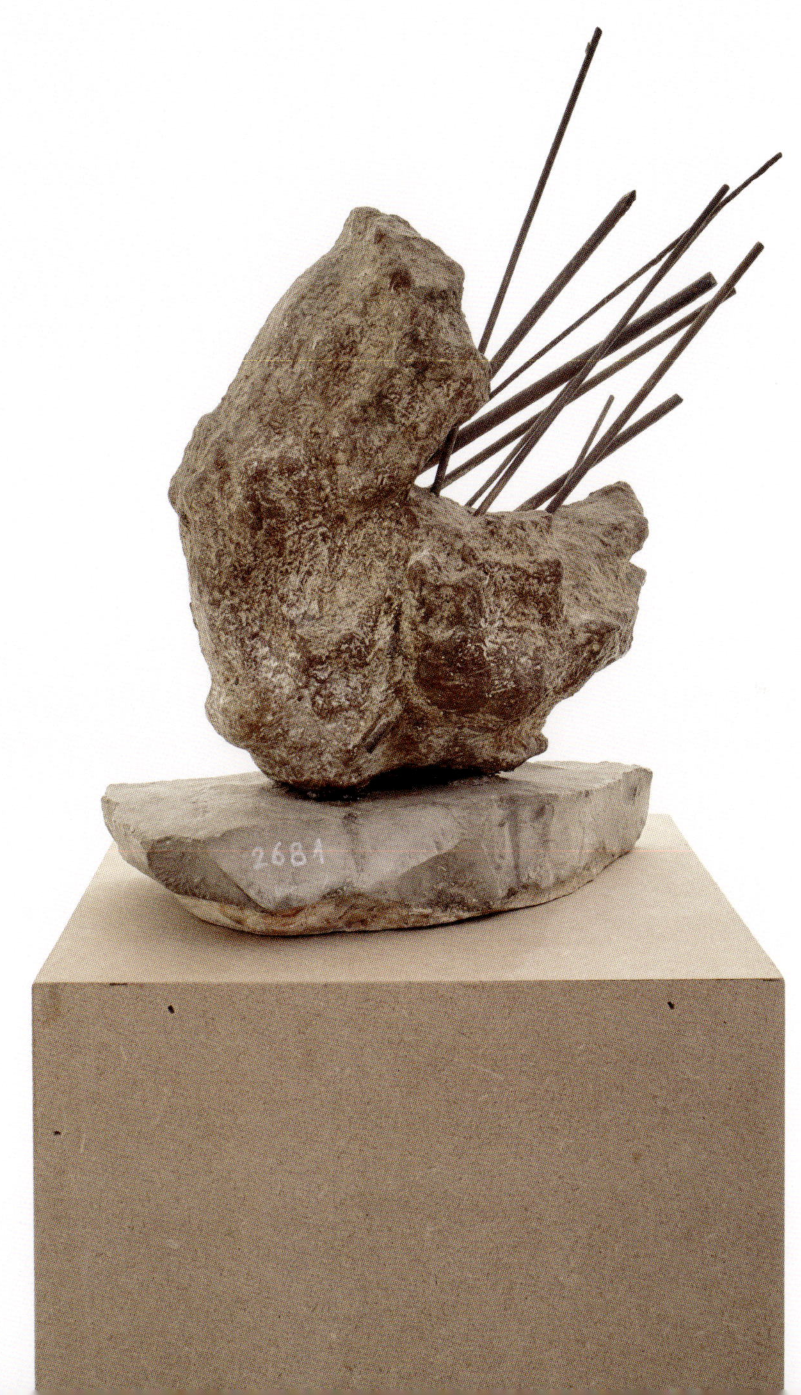

Olga Jevrić
Spacial Composition

Handel Street Projects, London
28 June–31 October 2019

table from left to right

Articulation of Space V, 1956
Ferric oxide, iron, 7.5 × 10.5 × 9.5 cm

Memento I, 1956
Ferric oxide, iron, 20 × 18 × 8.5 cm

Articulation of Space IV (Grasshopper), 1958
Ferric oxide, iron, 30 × 25 cm

Vertical Composition, 1956
Cement, iron, 18 × 9 × 6.5 cm

Memento II, 1956
Fired glazed clay, 19 × 14 × 4 cm

Three Elements Ib, 1956
Iron, 19 × 28 × 16 cm

Mine, 1956
Ferric oxide, gypsum, iron, 30.5 × 16.5 × 12 cm

fireplace from left to right

Proposal for a Monument, Prokuplje, 1951
Cement, 23.5 × 23.5 × 11.5 cm

Proposal for a Monument, Prokuplje, 1951
Dried earth, 24 × 24 × 12 cm

corner

Portrait RD, 1952
Gypsum, 28 × 40 × 36 cm

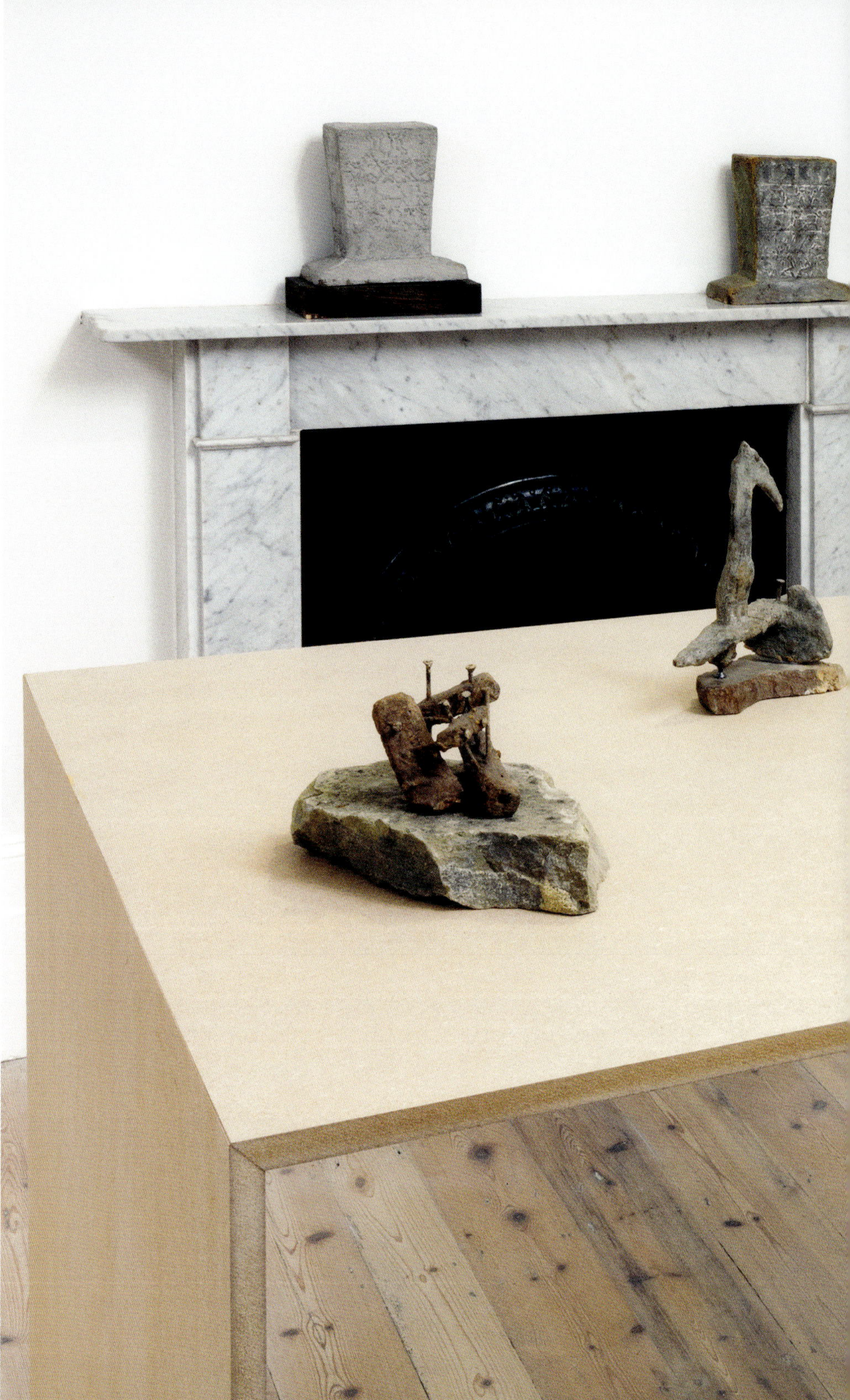

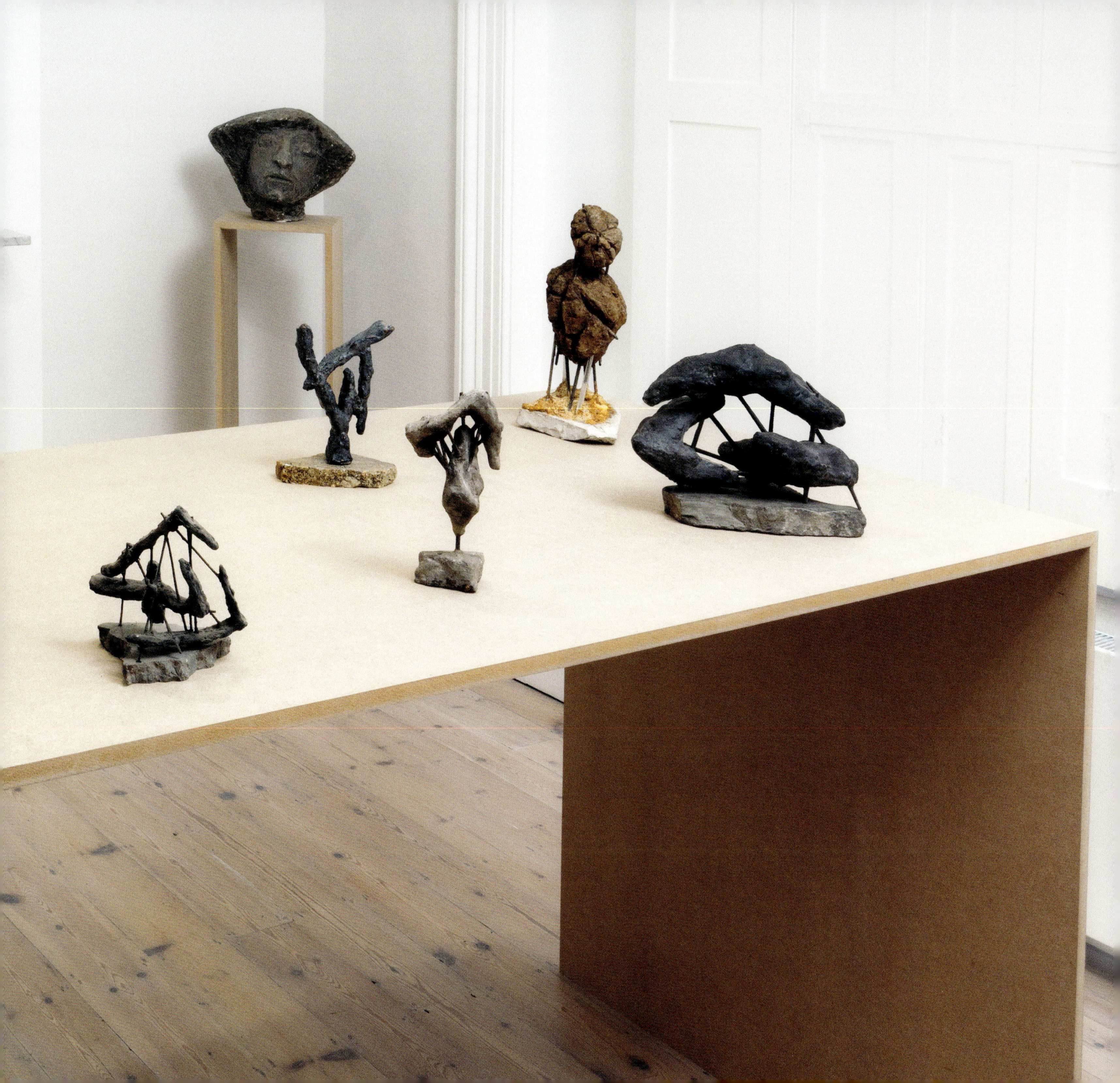

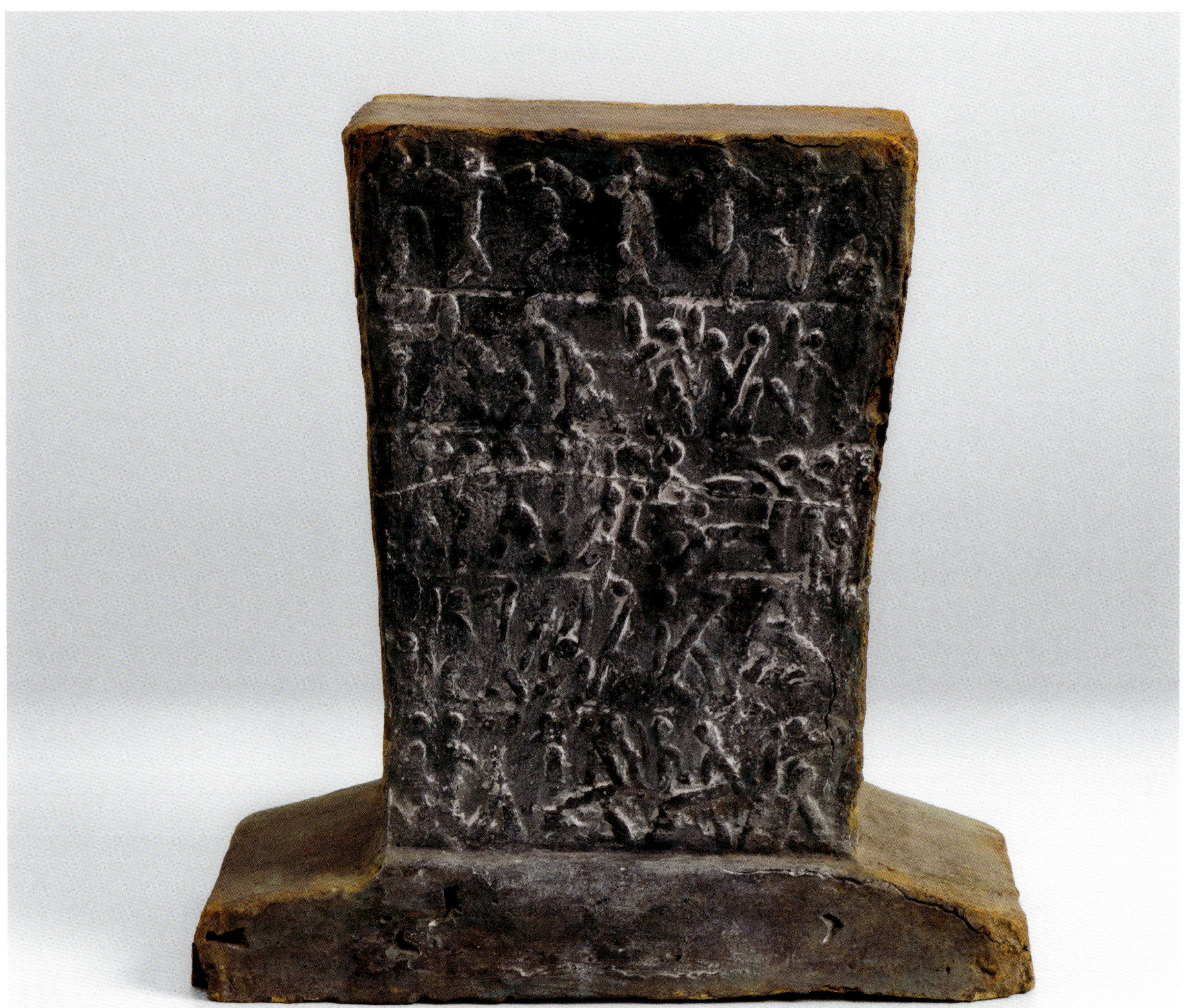

left

Proposal for a Monument, Prokuplje, 1951
Dried earth, 24 × 24 × 12 cm

right

Relief on the Theme of Reconstruction, 1948
Patinated gypsum, 40 × 28.3 × 1.5 cm

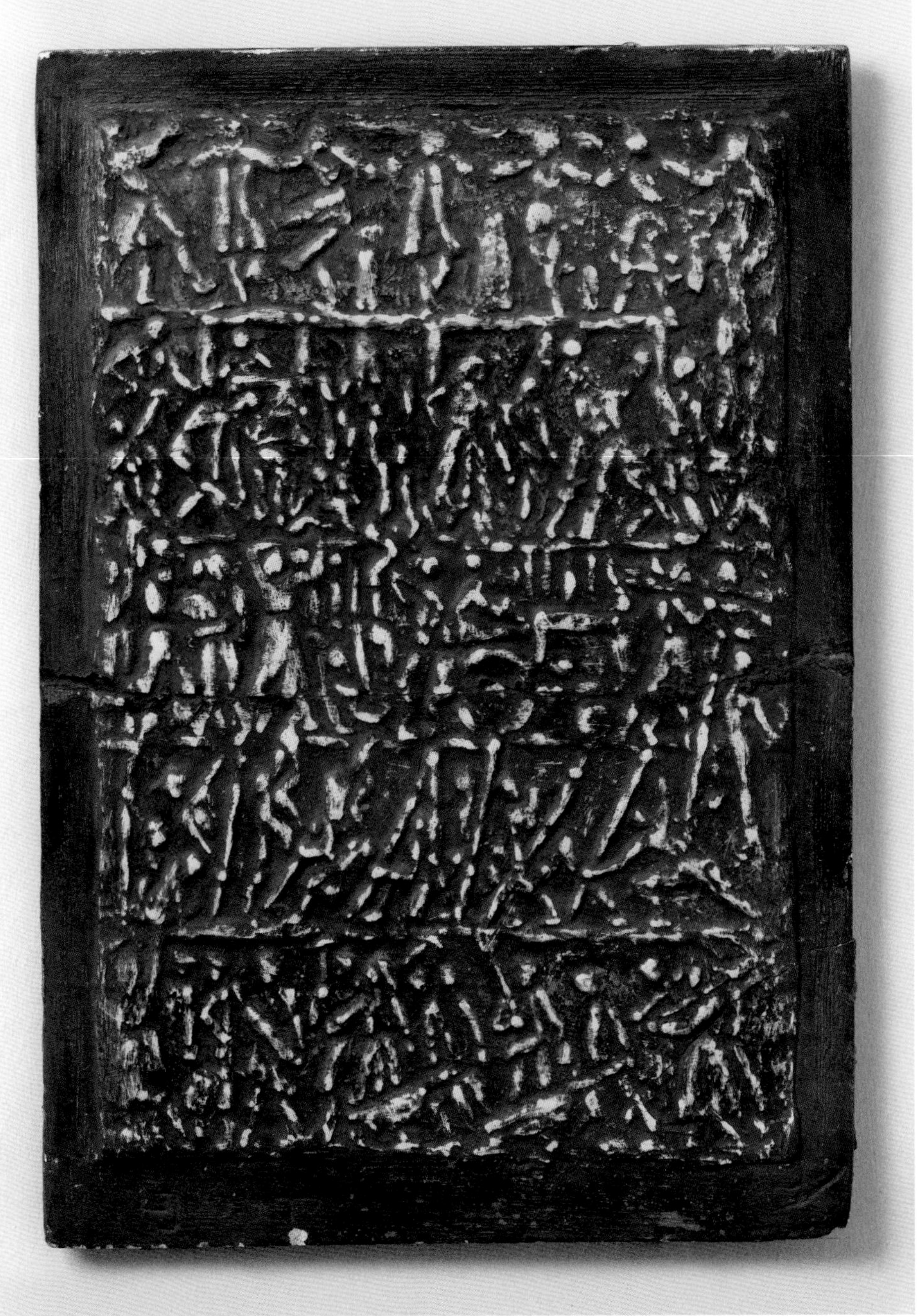

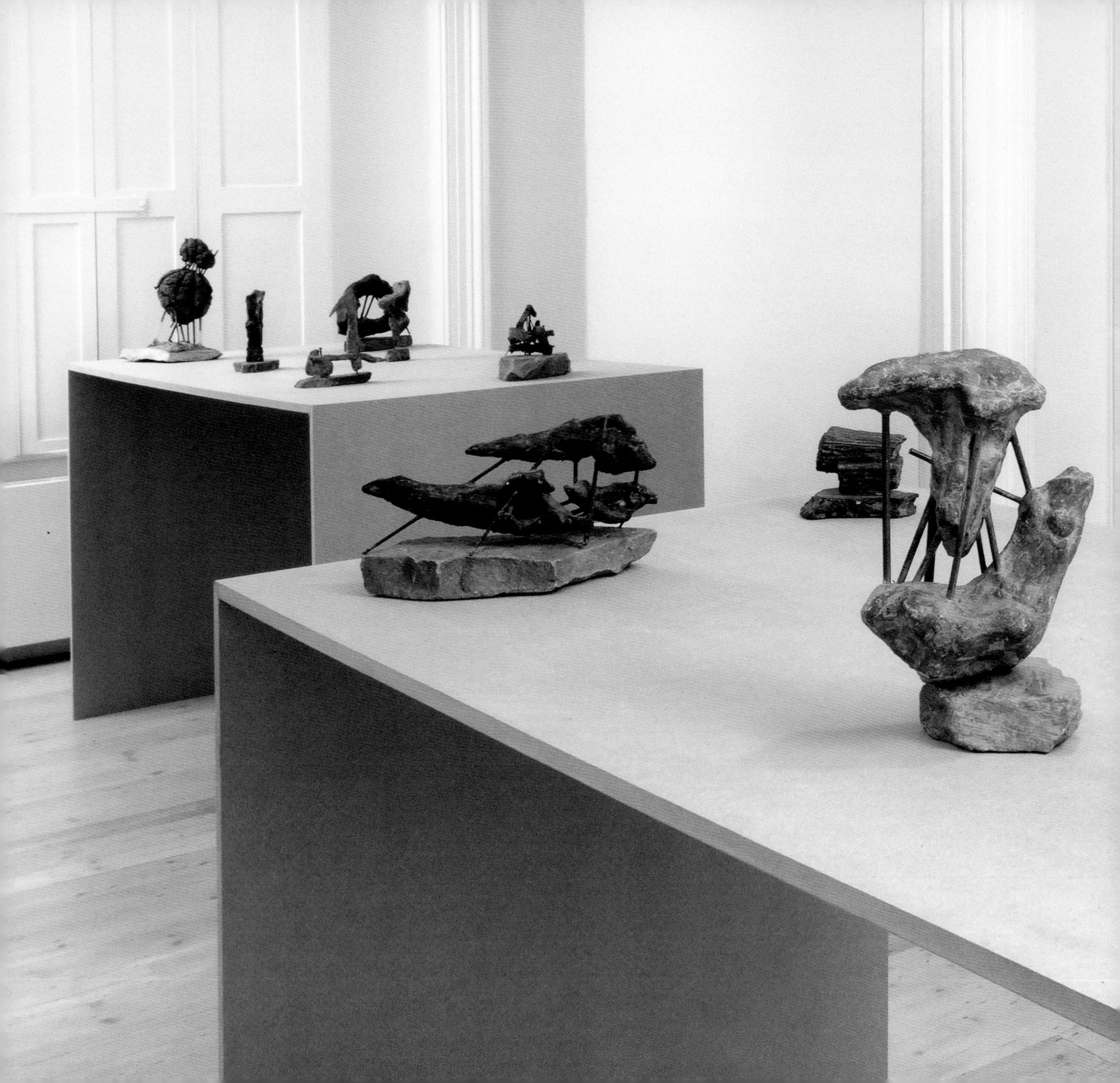

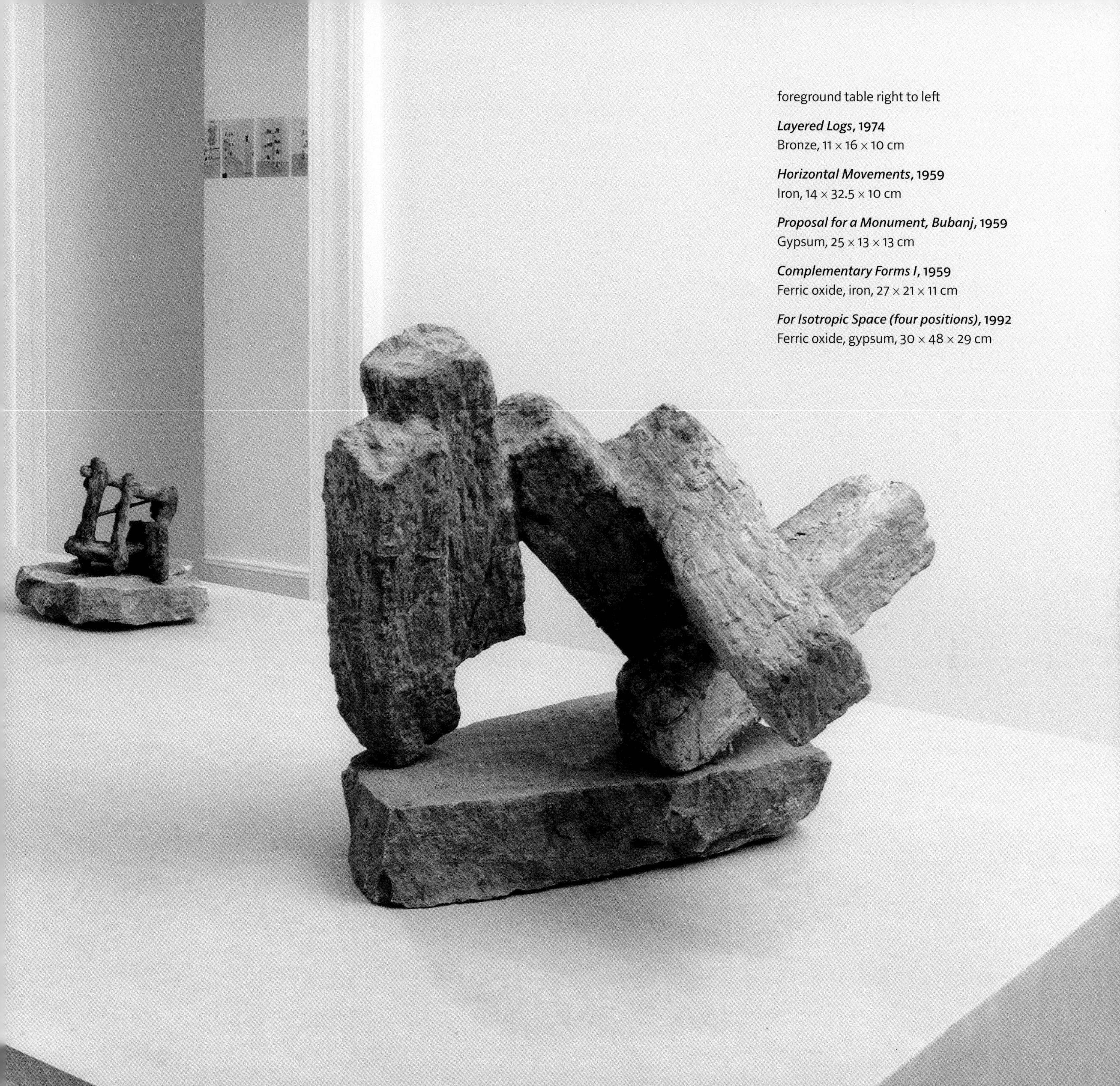

foreground table right to left

Layered Logs, 1974
Bronze, 11 × 16 × 10 cm

Horizontal Movements, 1959
Iron, 14 × 32.5 × 10 cm

Proposal for a Monument, Bubanj, 1959
Gypsum, 25 × 13 × 13 cm

Complementary Forms I, 1959
Ferric oxide, iron, 27 × 21 × 11 cm

For Isotropic Space (four positions), 1992
Ferric oxide, gypsum, 30 × 48 × 29 cm

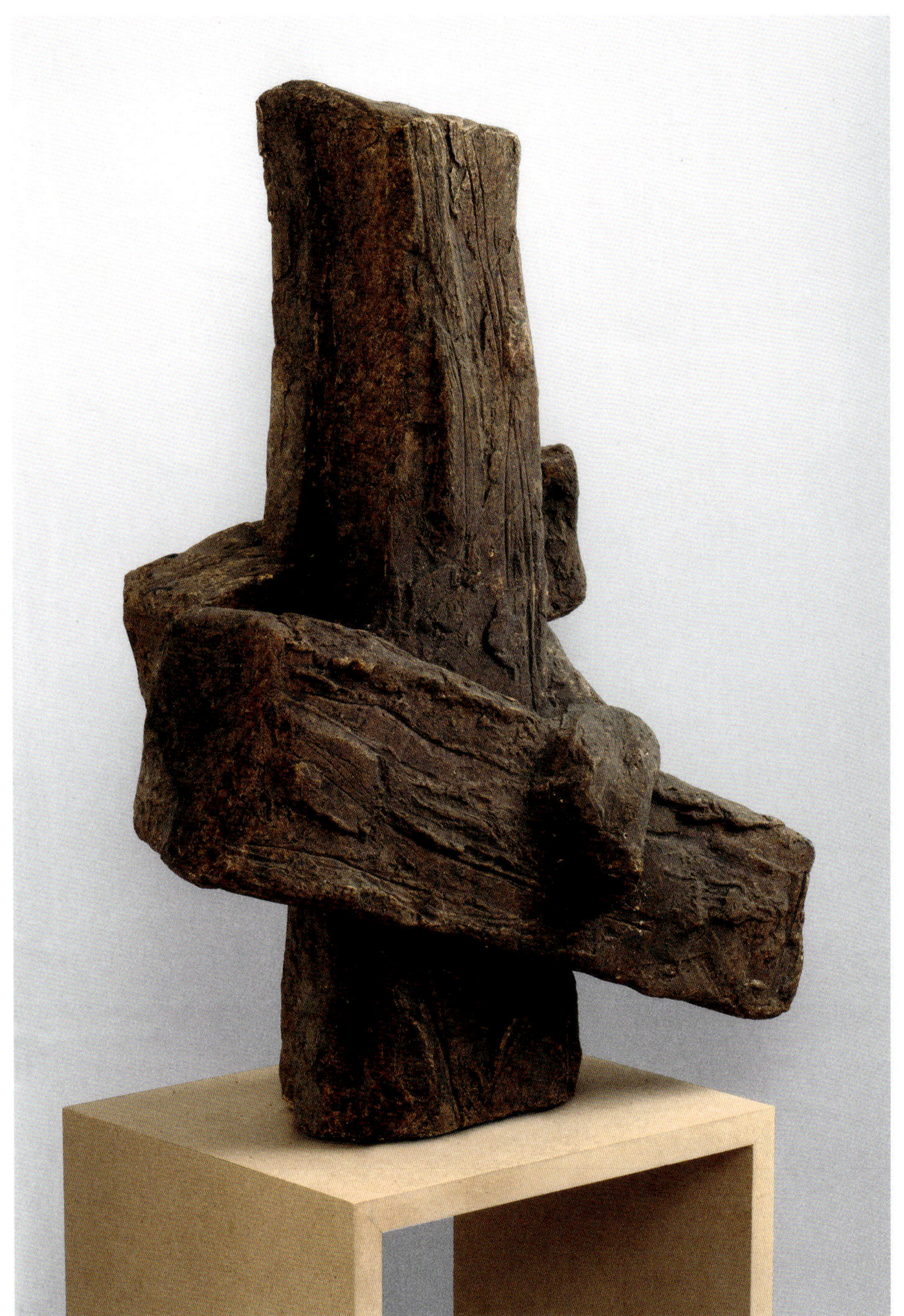

left

Big Crossing, 1987
Ferric oxide, gypsum, 52 × 44 × 20 cm

right

Portrait RD, 1952
Gypsum, 28 × 40 × 36 cm

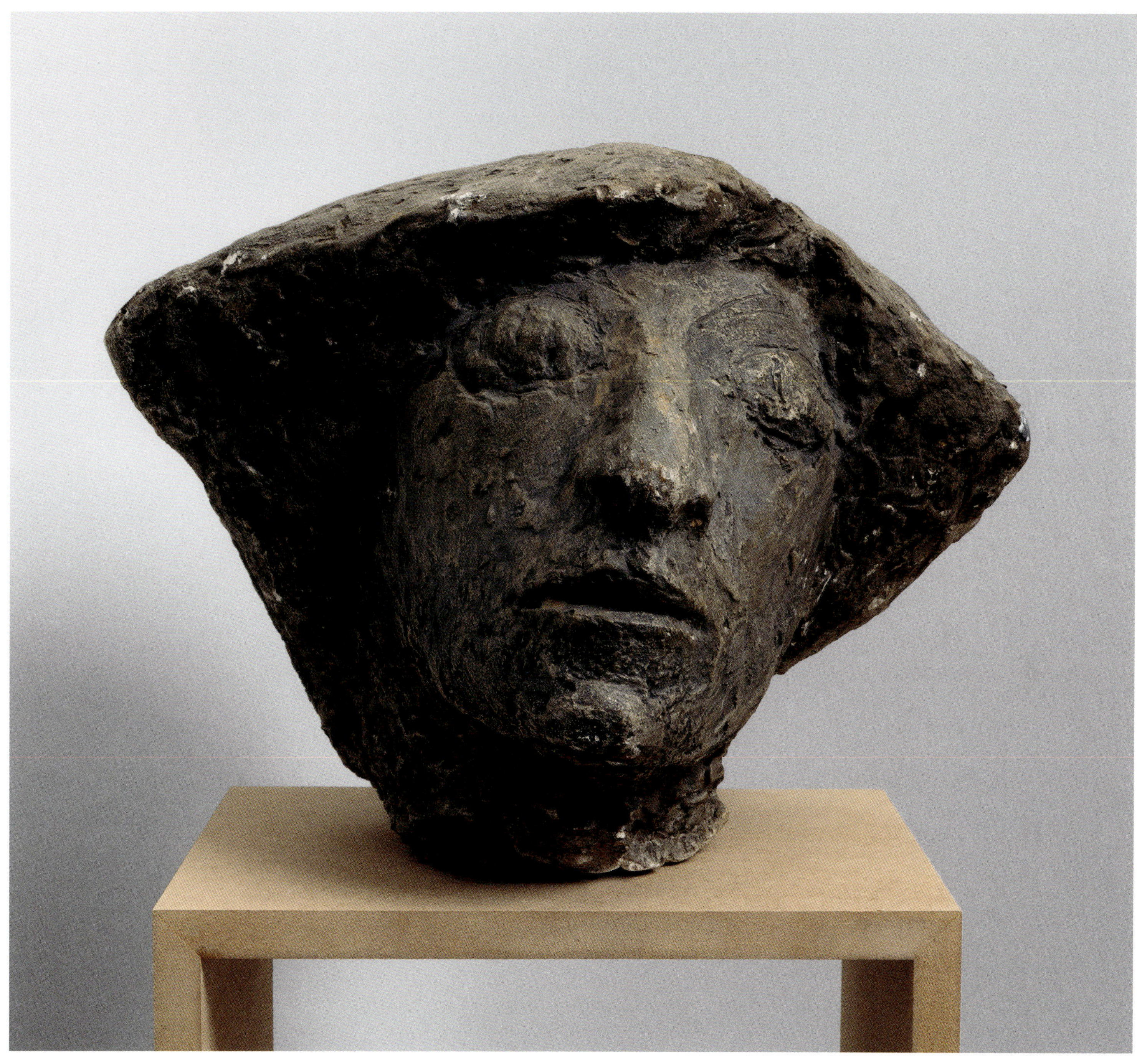

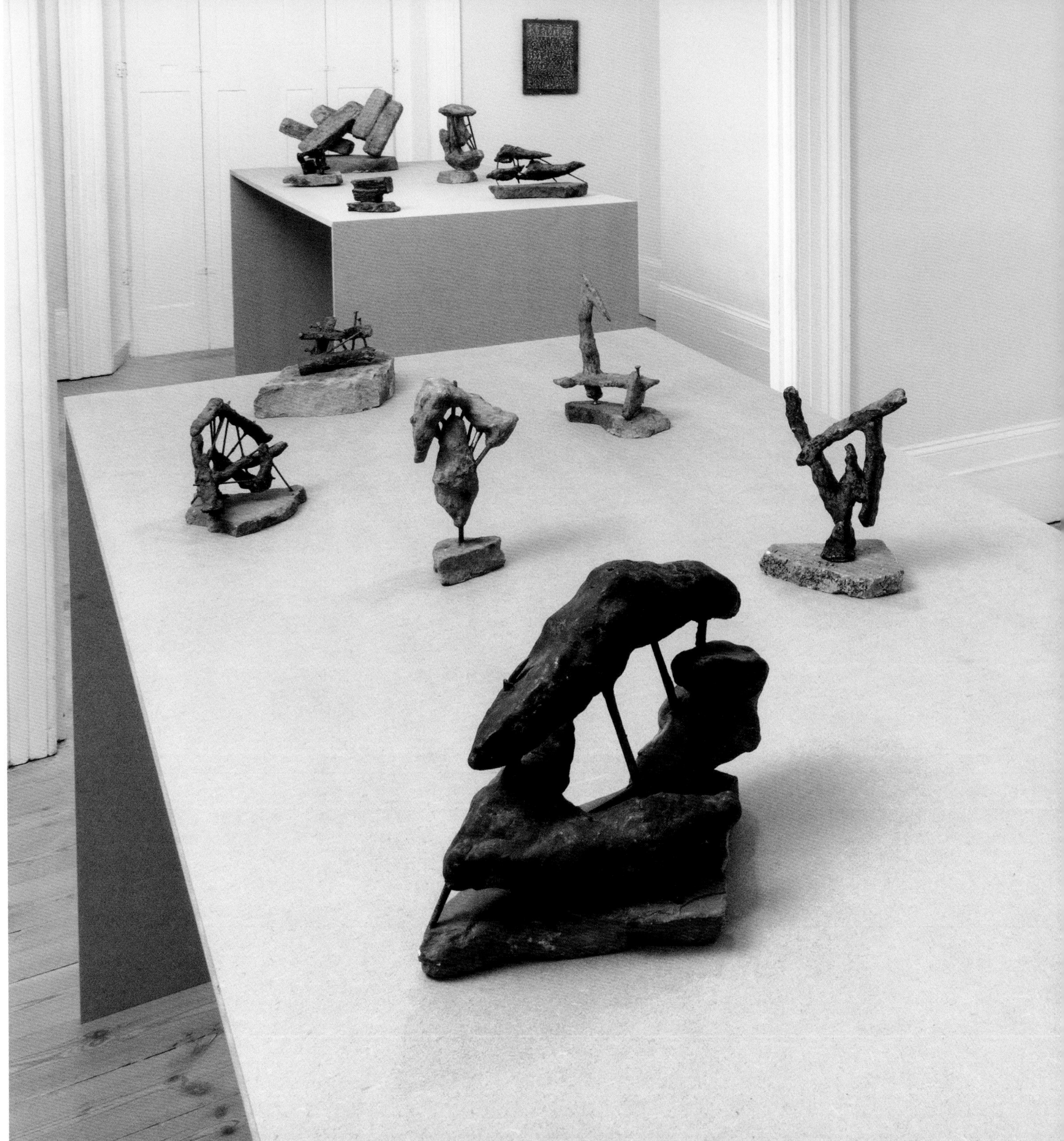

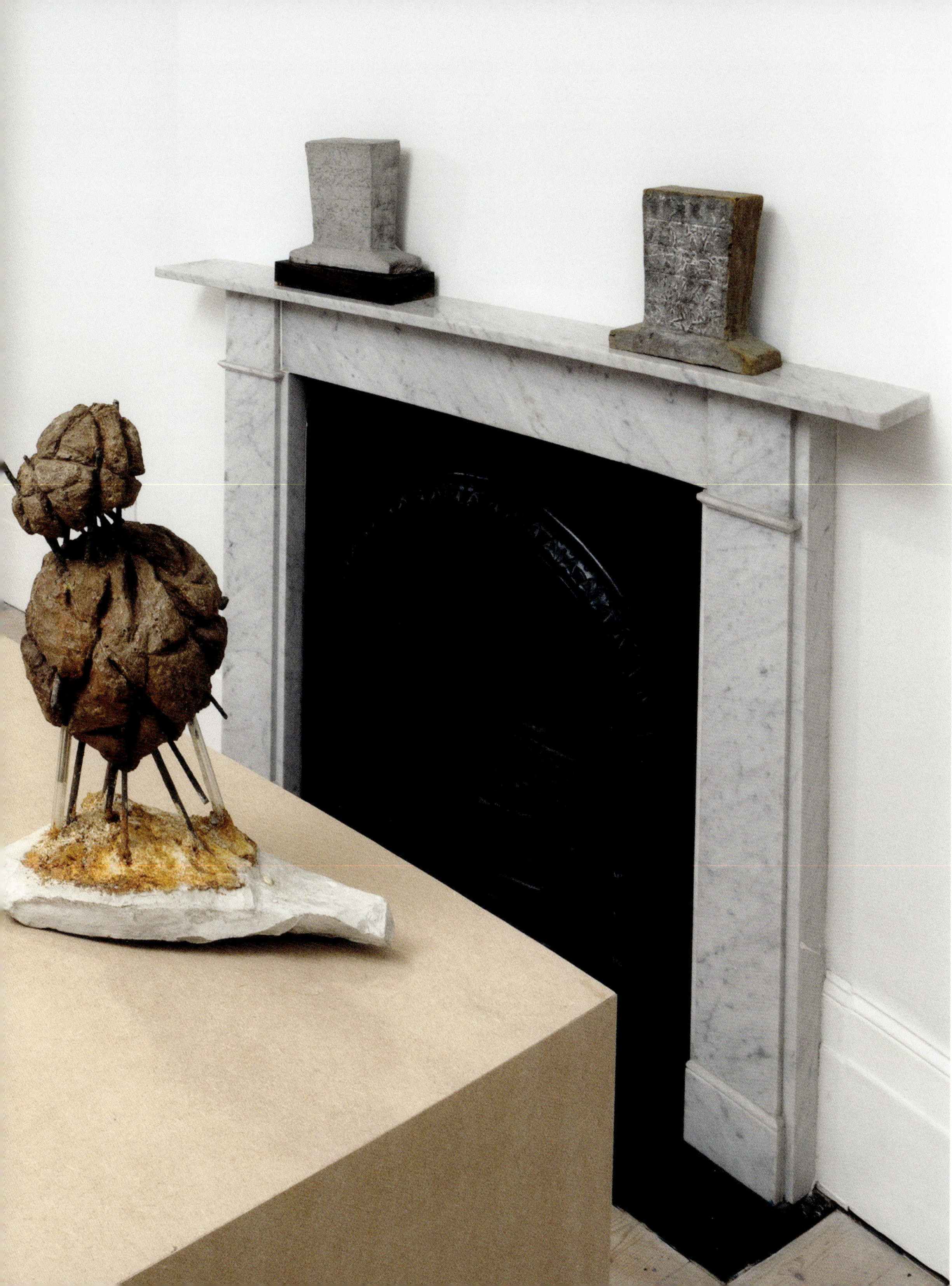

foreground table from right to left

Mine, 1956
Ferric oxide, gypsum, iron
30.5 × 16.5 × 12 cm

Three Elements Ib, 1956
Iron, 19 × 28 × 16 cm

Memento II, 1956
Fired glazed clay, 19 × 14 × 4 cm

Vertical Composition, 1956
Cement, iron, 18 × 9 × 6.5 cm

*Articulation of Space IV
(Grasshopper)*, 1958
Ferric oxide, iron, 30 × 25 cm

Memento I, 1956
Ferric oxide, iron, 20 × 18 × 8.5 cm

Articulation of Space V, 1956
Ferric oxide, iron, 7.5 × 10.5 × 9.5 cm

fireplace from right to left

Proposal for a Monument, Prokuplje,
1951
Dried earth, 24 × 24 × 12 cm

Proposal for a Monument, Prokuplje,
1951
Cement, 23.5 × 23.5 × 11.5 cm

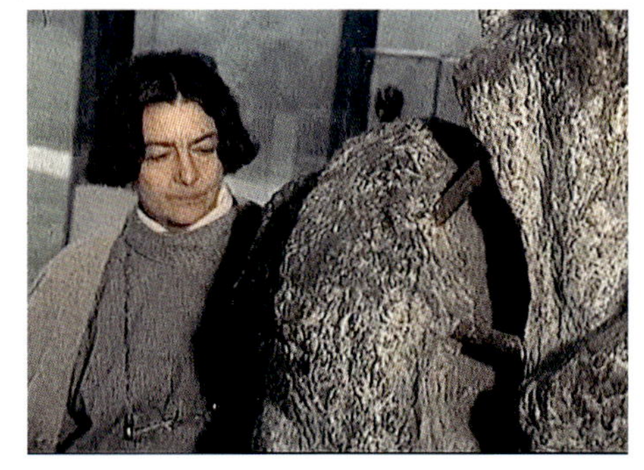
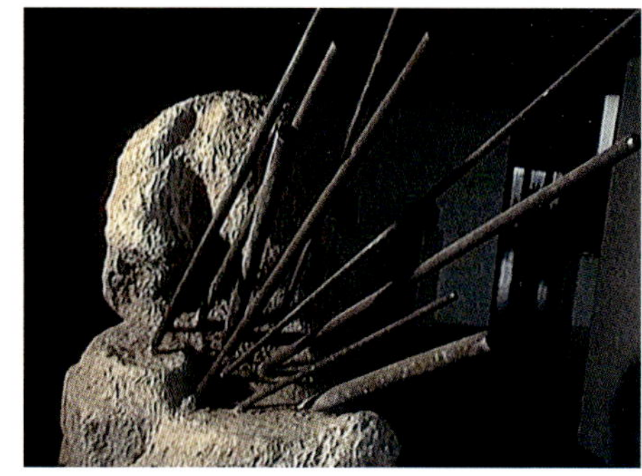
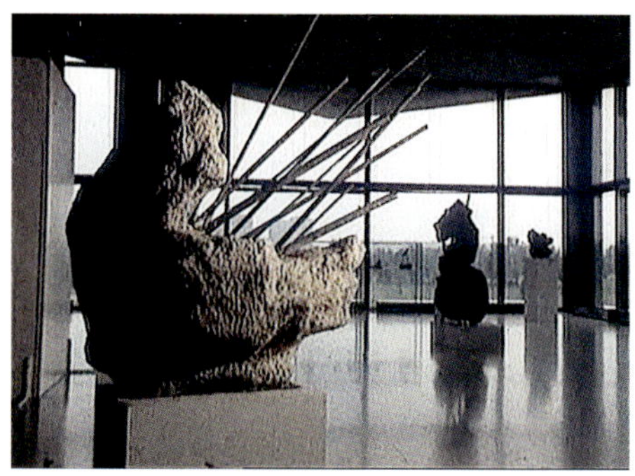
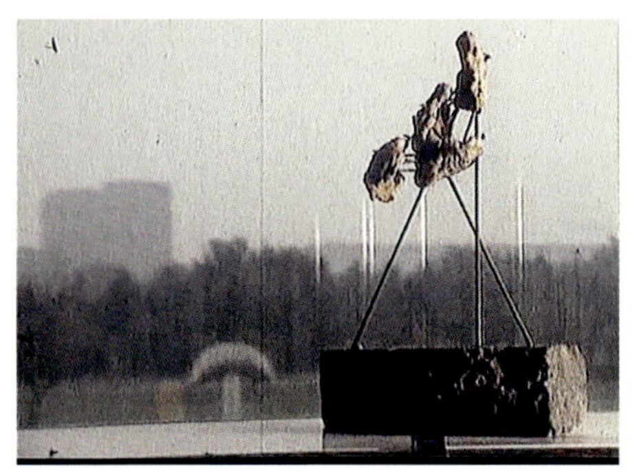
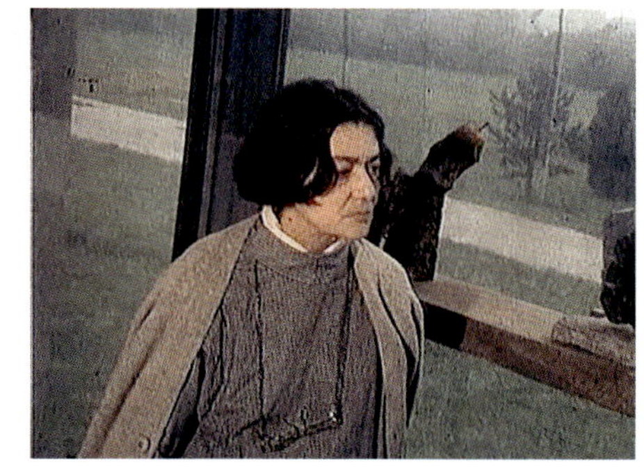
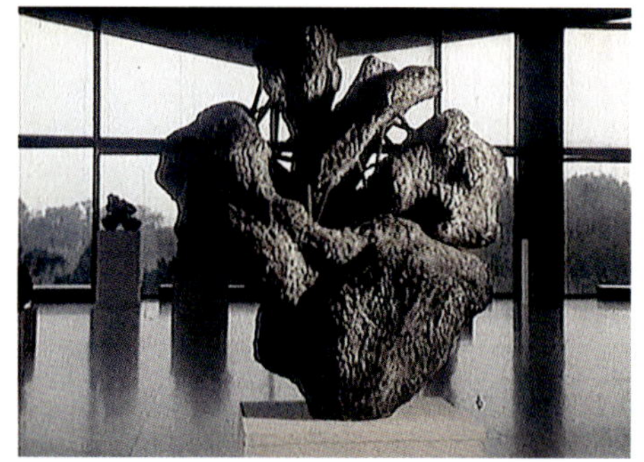
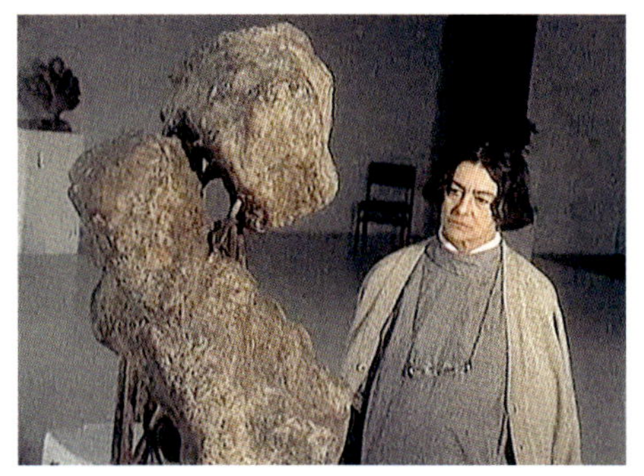
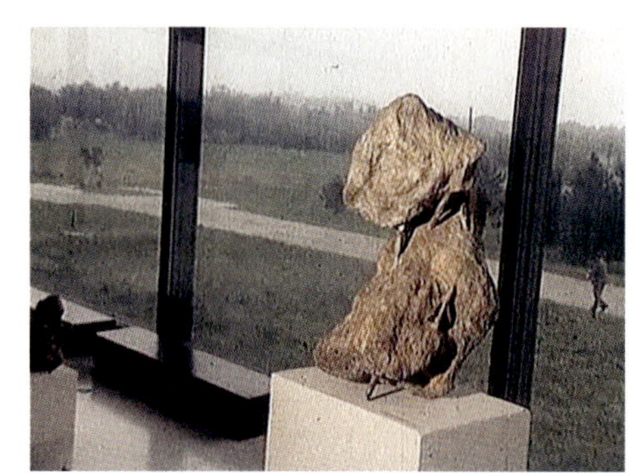
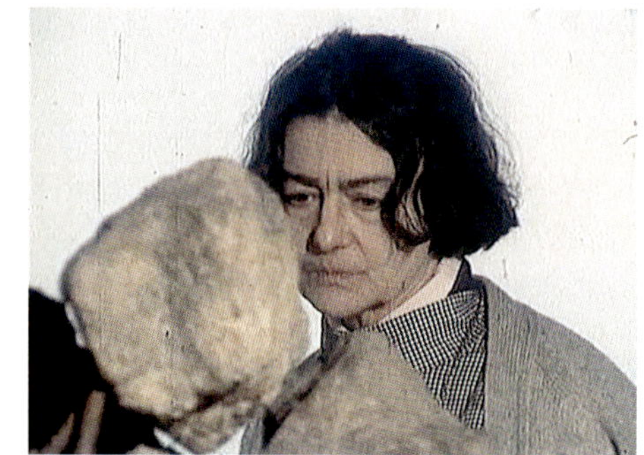
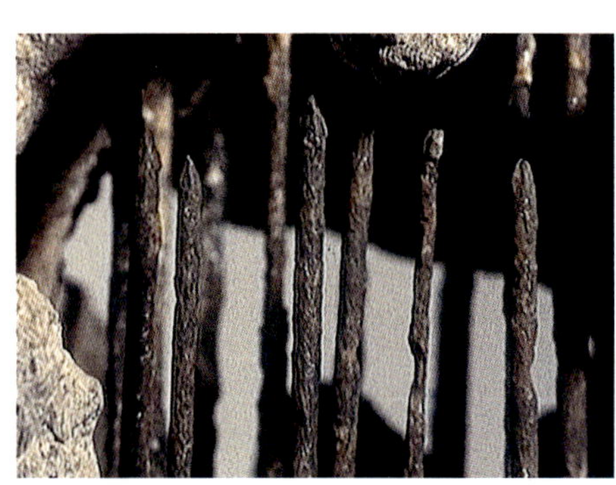
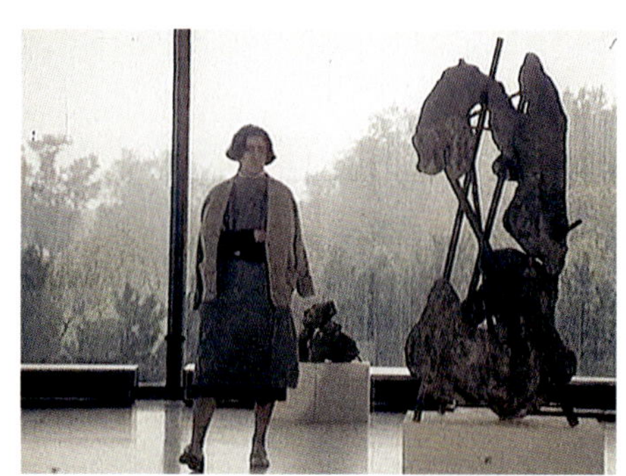
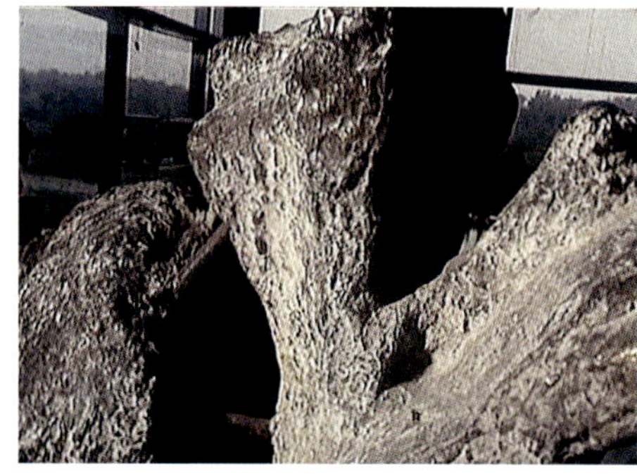

Olga Jevrić: Space and Time
transcription of artist's film voiceover

My world, our world, is in motion, in flux.
It exists in the dark and in the light, in the destruction and construction, decay and growth.
It is recognised in the coming together of paradox.
This difference is contained, overcome and erased by the realization of unity and harmony.
I use material as a means. I am not subservient to the material.

Like all artists, I use material to communicate and shape emotional and intellectual subjects,
as much as reflect on life experiences.

A number of factors have influenced the choice of materials.

These can be pragmatic and banal – a result of circumstance – or that specific properties of
materials contribute to the intensification of basic creative ideas.

For instance, I feel more familiarity with materials that, by their physical properties, allow for
precipitation of layers,

a procedure that is similar to the process of dispersion and formation of shapes in nature.

With any particular material I attempt to extract and emphasise those properties that suit my
primary impulse.
My substance is austere, unlikable, untamed, true in its physical determination.
I avoid situations where the value of the material might take on itself the value of the form and
its internal expression.
For me, it is of paramount importance to discover those moments through sculpture that
conquer the power of speech.

Film stills from 'Olga Jevrić:
Space and Time', 1982

Such moments embody the power of the message, and carry within it the suggestion of my
inner reason.

In the mythologies of almost all nations, light is experienced as the secret of life.

In the work of every creator, the myth of becoming develops through indicating the
separation of light from darkness.
Light here is both a physical and metaphysical substance; it provides the possibility for
discovery and revelation.
In landscape as in sculpture, it illuminates the hills, penetrates the ground and the gorges
as darkness, changes its shape and reveals unpredictable events that originate from its
movement.

In another sense, the secret of my forms is in the light of the one that comes from an
unknown direction in conversation with the secrets of the world.

The music I experience is the combination of sound masses, silences and interstices, to
produce melodic phrasing that span over time and through space.

The particularity of all these complex interrelations contains a statement, a reason for
activating sound as a creative medium.

All of this is analogous to the core and nature of my sculptural language.
My method rests on the construction of composite units.
No constitutive factor is itself an artistic event for itself.

The sculpture is formed from the interconnection of all the complex relations that lay behind
its creation.

In my work over the last 30 years, I have remained consistent in following this method to
create unique complexities of formal relationships, and not to repeat myself.
My sculptural principles are based on the complex linkage of all artistic elements.
What is more, these elements are always in motion and under question.

Spatial presence, the action and specific intrinsic qualities of the different materials I use
provide me with an infinity of possibilities that I can then exploit.

One means of identifying a resolution of the relationships between different masses within
my sculpture is provided by transferring the action to the iron rods, which in its movement
and interconnectedness and measures, also allow this concept to be invigorated with new
modulations and sustain its purpose.

Olga Jevrić's exhibition
at the Museum of
Contemporary Art,
Belgrade, 1981–2

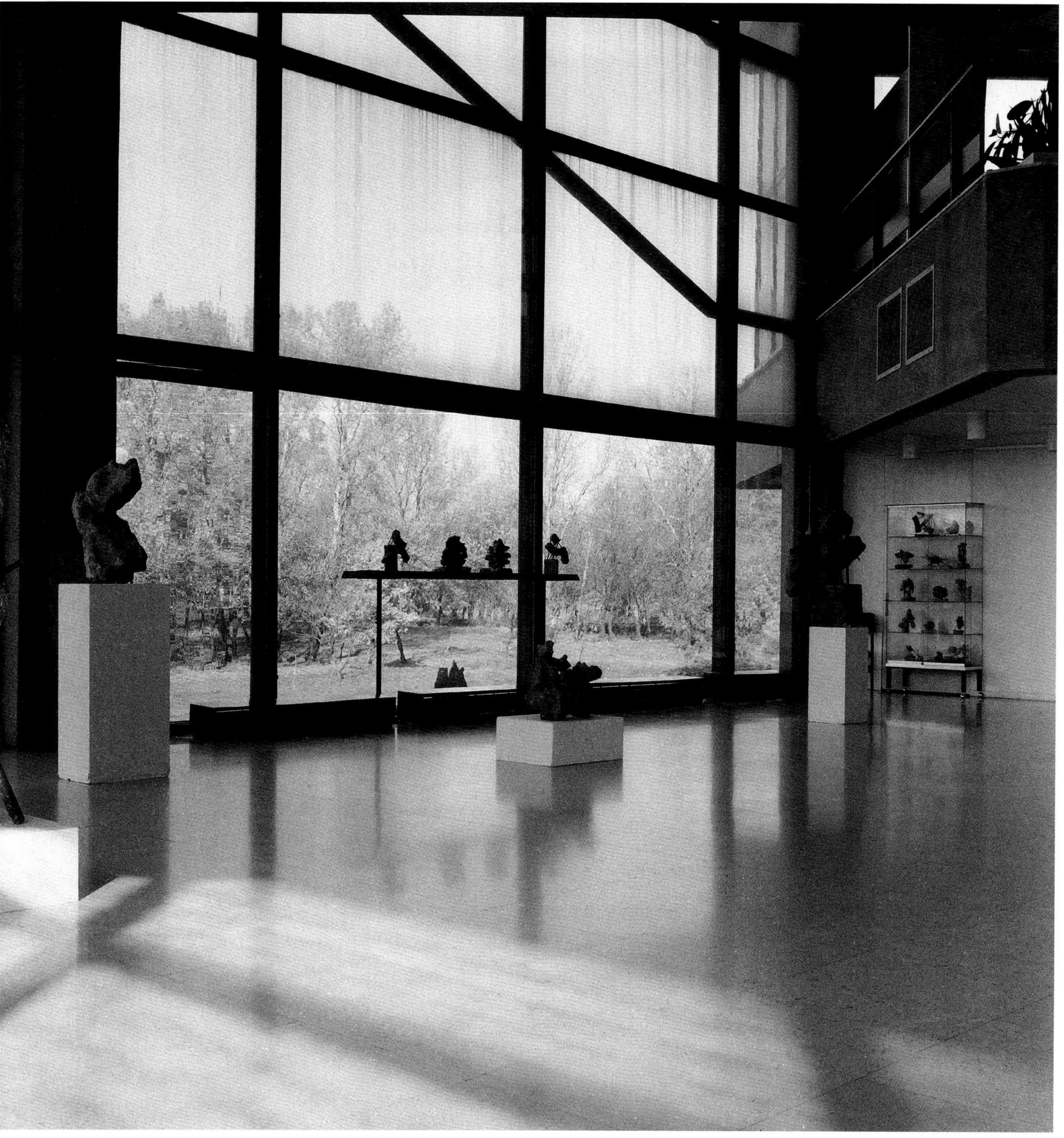

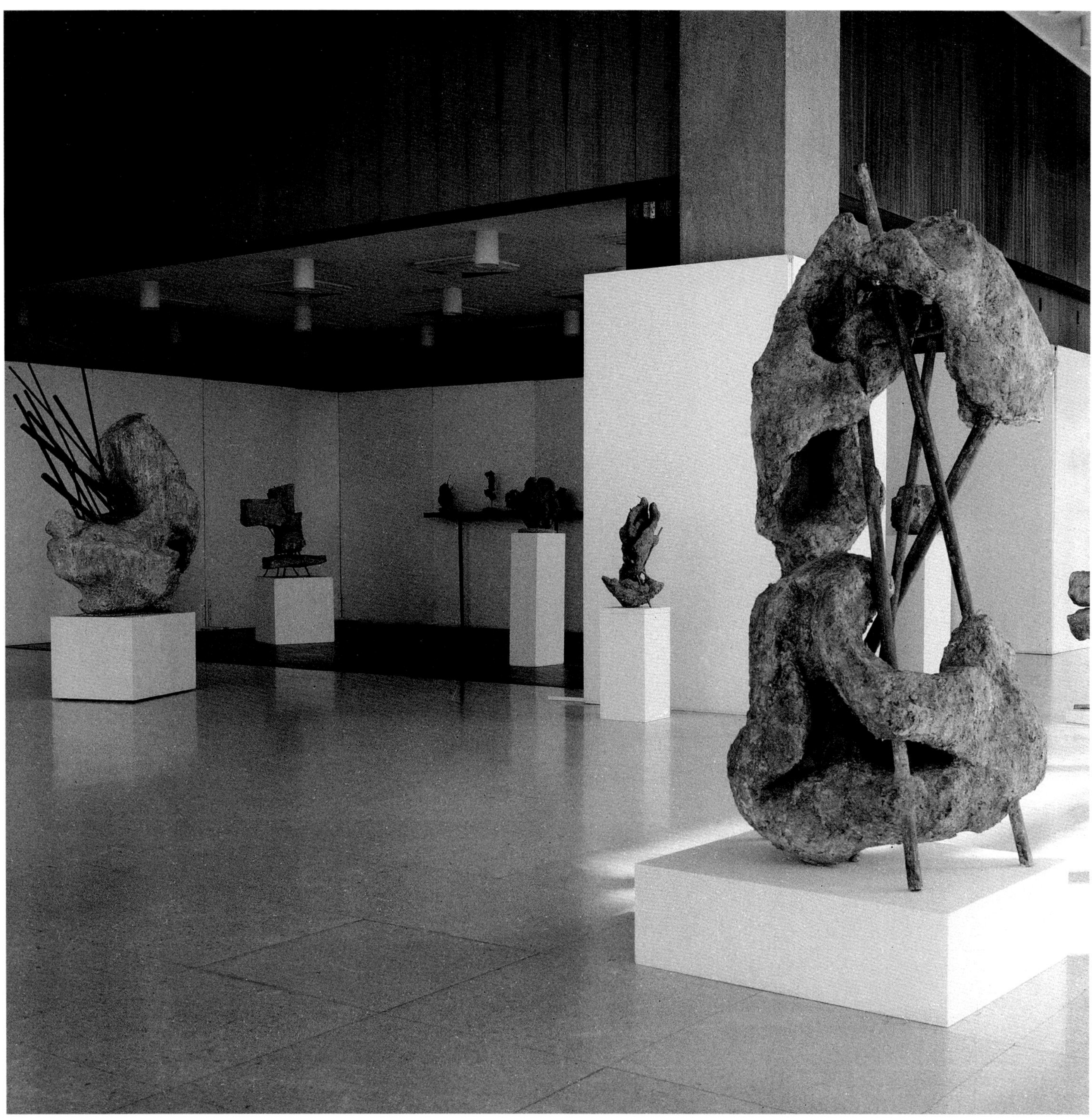

This is all at the heart of my sculpture.
There is also mass and volume, drawing and plasticity, plan and proportional relationships,
rhythms and contours, and compositional structure.
All of this together contributes to the subject of my work.

Each component is essential, yet the expressive subject of each work is communicated by each
aspect of the system working together.

From a spiritual perspective, time is circling, every present moment touches somewhere that
time - and before time.

I travel to the end of infinity towards the new beginning.

To watch: https://vimeo.com/344576753
All stills on p.78 are taken from *Olga Jevrić: Space and Time*, 16mm film (digitised).
Directed by Dragomir Zupanc, produced by Dunja Blažević, camerawork by Veselin Krčmar.
Filmed at the artist's exhibition at the Museum of Contemporary Art, Belgrade, 1982
Made for Belgrade TV, 1982. Length: six minutes

Soundtrack: 'Come in Number 51, Your Time is Up', Pink Floyd, 1970
This version was used for the film *Zabriskie Point*, original version: 'Careful with That Axe,
Eugene', 1968

Olga Jevrić's exhibition at the
Museum of Contemporary Art,
Belgrade, 1981–2

43 Theses
Olga Jevrić

1. relation: mass – space – bar
2. cusa sine qua non (cause – in – fact): conditionality and conditional
3. rhythm
4. movement
5. being in space
6. duel with gravity
7. problem of balance
8. formation
9. clash: organic form – rigidity of mechanical shape
10. articulation of the space – activation in the terms of medium
11. mass as a carrier of activity
12. expression on basis of analogous exteriorisation of psychogenic elements
13. unity of opposites
14. the effect of the force of gravity
15. two – way axial movement
16. correlation of nodal points
17. tension
18. nothing is indifferent – everything is relative
19. sum of actions – poly psychogenicity
20. quantity – new quality
21. destruction – reconstruction
22. the problem of the failed collision
23. national modul
24. measure – dosing quantities

25. trauma
26. irrational – rational
27. emotional – intellectual
28. technical civilisation – primordial force
29. conscious – intuitive
30. speed of the line movement
31. tilt – angle
32. vulnerability – fear
33. right place – tuned sound
34. sound
35. incarceration
36. polymorphic
37. profiling – variability
38. time
39. mathematical principles
40. flows of drills
41. concave – convex continuities
42. direction
43. angle

Metaphoric of dialectical thought, themes:
unity of organic and inorganic; biological and tectonic (in morphology);
psychism and animism; activity of the mass which has all predicates
of potential human activity; force – physical laws as separate entities
brought in by metaphor of the form; problem of the classical harmony in
the illusion of disharmony; juncture of rational and irrational, thoughtful
and emotional, lyrical and dramatic – tragic; national modul – spirit of
Balkans; unity of objective and subjective; juncture of subconscious and
over – me; juncture of relative and absolute; unified field; existences and
mysteries; negation of negation; anti-abstraction; speech of the form;
movement of opposing forms; matter: metaphor of anthropo – psycho-
morphic events; primordial and today's; destruction and superstructure;
prevailed tragic; struggle for survival – resistance to negation; resistance
to destructive; split – complementarity; energy, movement, change
(phenomenology of human experience)

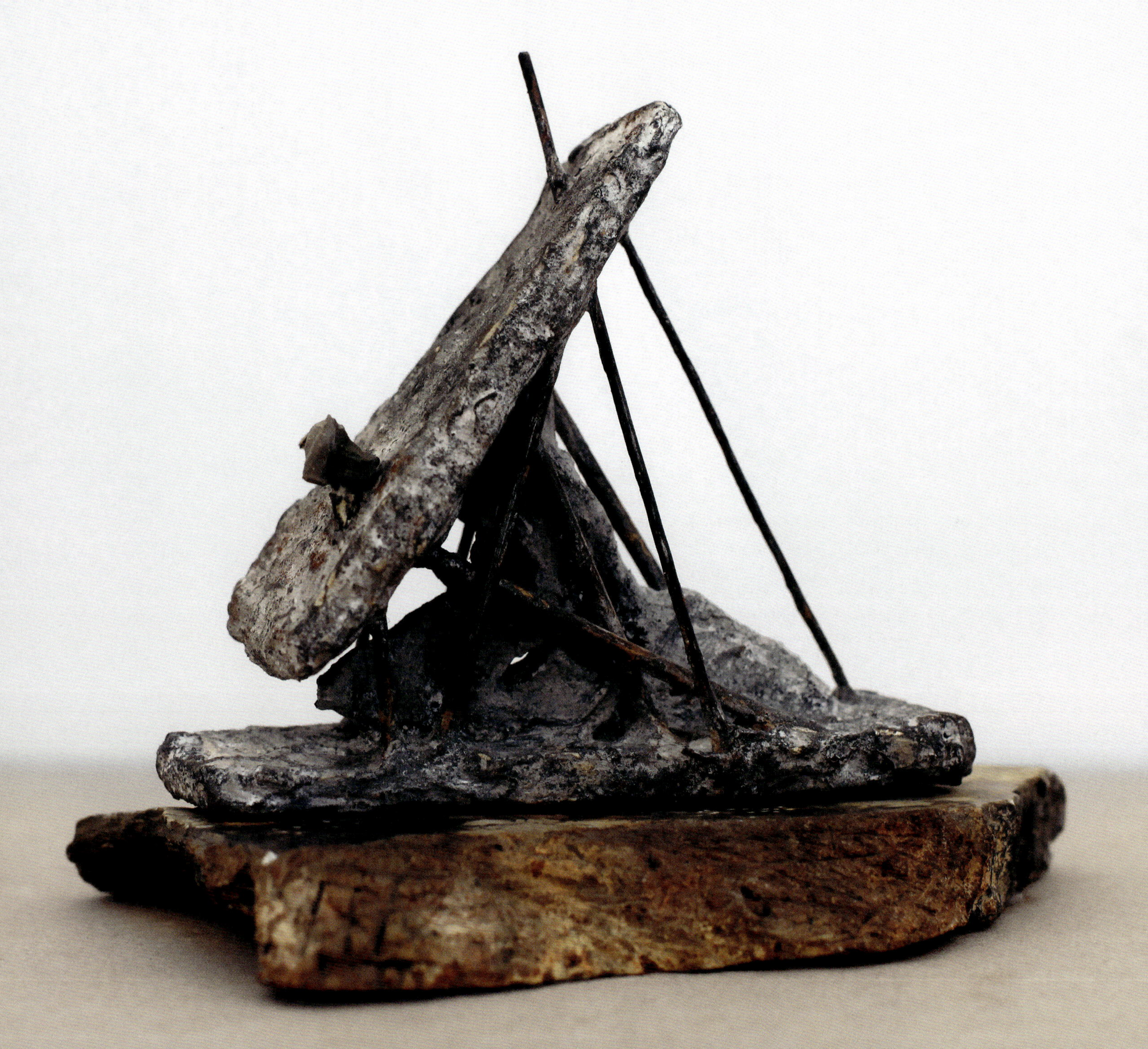

Olga Jevrić sculptures, 1950–1970

Joan Key

Thesis 22: The problem of the failed collision

The above quotation is from Olga Jevrić's '43 Theses'. There is a further list, of 'Unities', and together these documents effectively form a manifesto outlining the concerns of an abstract sculptural practice.[1] Although the influence of a spectrum of theories underlying doctrinal modernism is evident, the lists do not define sculpture's aims but arrange terms associated with its making in a series of loose comparisons. This methodology implies that no term is absolute so there is no collision of meanings in the sense of direct oppositions or exclusions. Jevrić's 'theses' and 'unities' do not work in a programmatic way but propose interactions between emotional, conceptual and material forces. The imagination of 'a failure to collide', for example, bears neither specific visual reference to how a sculpture might appear nor any practical indication about how to make it. Rather, it suggests a dramatic principle: of anticipation, that something will emerge, that space is held open for sculpture to achieve form on its own terms.

'Failed collision' is a significant idea within the drama of Jevrić's sculpture, a possibility whose dangerous influence is mitigated by a positive emphasis on connections or 'unities'. This produces a complex formality, inflected by philosophical and spiritual intuitions immanent to material and its processing.[2] There is little association with design or drawing practice. Actual holding, the contemplation of substance through touch, is a constant imaginative and theoretical resource for the numinous qualities of this work. For example, the possible 'unity of psychism and animism' may fail to make sense but may still inform speculation in practice. The interest in how the flow of thoughts may be materialised through process produces a sense of perpetual movement around and through the sculpture. This diversion suggests a traumatic element to be managed. Thesis 25, 'trauma', and Thesis 38, 'time', are markedly singular terms in Jevrić's lists, which are generally less specific and defined, for example the unities of: 'Juncture of rational and irrational, thoughtful and emotional, lyrical and dramatic-tragic'. These ideas remain in

Proposal for a Monument, Zev, 1958

dialogical relations throughout Jevrić's practice, not in order to find compromise but to mobilise amorphous forms to render an unrepresentable intermediate state of abstraction.

Structure does not mean that collision is impossible. It remains latent, as potential, or as the aftermath of sculptural activity, operating equally on an intimate and a cosmic scale. Empirical observation interfaces with emotional proximities as Jevrić works directly with the experience of moment-by-moment relations to surfaces. The immediacy of making and imagining the becoming forms allows sculptural ideas to retain fluidity until their developmental urgencies can stop. The tensions that occur between material and somatic content haunt Jevrić's practice. Crucial to this tension, in Jevrić's case, is the paradoxical desire for monumentality in abstraction. If a monument's subject cannot be directly represented, the concept of asserting the essence of some timeless value becomes embodied within abstract form. This permanence of value may be an aspiration, but one which ultimately fails in a modernist context concerned with the flux of everyday life, the meanings of commodity fetishism and a pressure towards future progress that renders any present state in danger of almost immediately being 'out of date'.

The perpetual movement of 'failure to collide' can then be a positive emotion generated by sculpture, especially in a period when a history of conflict means that monuments are longed for but impossible. Traditionally, monuments are established in confrontation with the viewer: dignified frontality, a stable base, proportionate build, impressive scale. Jevrić's work engages

with the possibility of transience in monumental projects where it is difficult to fix an outline or a core, or to find an ideal place from which to see the sculpture. Formlessness becomes a value: a concrete lumpenness. In this state abstract resolution remains ungrasped, existing as relative to indeterminate spatial components held within the remit of the sculpture. The dynamics of these spaces are viewed as equal to and reciprocally formed by the sculpture's material content. A lack of condensed limits engages the monumental as transcending scale rather than as impressive scale of substance. Jevrić concentrates the viewer's thoughts into the invention of formal and informal spatial relationships rather than the weight of physical presence.

The sculptures on view in London were made in postwar Belgrade. Sculpture embodied a special purpose at this time in Europe, symbolising the positive energy of reconstruction without avoiding memory of the traumatically destructive events of the war.[3] This aspiration, to rescue positive values from disastrous global conflict, is represented by the internationalism of the biennale movement in which Jevrić's work was represented. Fragility and fragmentation – concepts of the *informel*[4] – become tentative aesthetic values that might counter the confident symbolic architecture and sculpture of fascism. The effect on abstract aesthetic judgement is one of sensitivity to subtle degrees of difference within distressed surfaces, and the politics of appreciation for nuanced formal distinctions and identifications. It was in this period that, for example, Clement Greenberg elaborated on the integrity of the relative uses of flatness in the fragmentation of Cubist collage, and on the pictorial surface as an overall planar structure to be protected from crisis.[5]

Jevrić uses techniques of modelling and spatial assemblage to consider how parts of sculpture may exist in a 'duel with gravity' (Thesis 6). The notion of duelling forces allows metaphysical speculation on failed collision, how 'space' both holds apart and participates in the forming of materials. On the atomic scale, an alchemical collision of elements or particles creates internalised energies, strange substances, explosions. Experimental failures with variations in timings and material process are part of alchemy, which always holds the possibility that a crossing of trajectories may occur too early or too late for the instantaneous transformation of base matter. Jacques Derrida describes how a lack of synchronous timing, a 'disjointure in the very presence of the present', a feeling that 'time is out of joint',[6] may activate speculation on some 'thing' that is capable of rearticulating the structures of the failed encounter that made its form possible.

As a dramatic example, Derrida analyses Hamlet's initial failure to be present with the presence of his father's spirit as 'anachrony' a breakdown of precedence, of justice in the universal temporal order:

What does not happen in this anachrony! Perhaps 'the time', time itself, precisely 'our time', the epoch and the world shared among us, ours everyday, nowadays, the present as our present. Especially when things are not going well among us … is not this disjuncture, this dis-adjustment of the 'it's going badly' necessary for the good, or at least the just, to be announced?[7]

Shakespeare positions the first ghostly event immediately at the opening of the play 'Hamlet', when the spirit of his father appears to soldiers on the ramparts. The need for just re-articulation in the aftermath of terrible deeds is subsequently mirrored and elaborated upon through thematic recurrences within the play: as emotional internal monologue, as persisting memory underlying dramatic action, as the dialogical forces of good and evil that structure narrative development and as a supernatural warning that will have a profound impact on the history of a royal line. Hamlet's initial failure to encounter this ghost, to ascertain the timing of the historic events this appearance portends, opens up a mobility of speculation about timing and revenance. The comparison being made with this disjointed timing and Jevrić's timing is rather one of resonance than potential repetition: there is not one single failed collision, but a preoccupation with the anticipation of collisions that provoke intimations of tragic consequence.

The visualisation and management of an unstable play of forces is reflected in Jevrić's use of materials. Articulated lumpen forms, modelled in layers of cement or plaster, interact with connective motifs: metallic reinforcing rods, pipes, nails. The forms can feel unquantifiable, strangely mobile or transformable. The rods interact in different ways with the modelling, leaving unresolved the question of what comes first. In traditional modelling there is a primary relation between external form and armature, but this is doubtful in the case of Jevrić's sculpture. Instead, it is as if flesh has been torn away from the skeleton beneath; a play of dynamic forces; an opening up to reveal an interior.[8] However, the sense of order in Jevrić's rods suggests their secondary presence, as additions acting on the gravity of the cement forms or holding devices that connect and transfer weight, an important somatic force.

Cement and plaster belong to the smooth cladding and suggestions of lightness in modernist architecture, but in Jevrić's work they become grey, cindery, tinted with ferric oxide that bleeds outward from the sculpture's granular interior to its external surfaces. This granularity holds an uncertain potential for hidden entropic change that further unsettles identification and resists formal values. Writing about the use of granularity and entropy in Robert Smithson's work, Rosalind Krauss observes that, for Smithson, 'entropy was less a condition of boundaries surmounted than a function of structural blindness'.[9] There is an element of blindness, too, in the entropic quality of timing in Hamlet's relation to the ghost. Jevrić's forms also exclude a consciousness of fixed sequential timing of visibility as alignments and horizons shift and twist, reveal and hide. The picturing of cement and exposed iron rods might be futuristic, but in her work they have more in common with the ruins that would have been evident in the surroundings of postwar Belgrade. This imagery has an obscene relation to modernist concerns with perfectible material and its satisfactory functionality.

The symbolism of iron and its uses brings other qualities: support, connectivity, measure, numeric quantity (Thesis 20: 'quantity, a new quality'), aggressive piercing, caging (Thesis 35: 'incarceration'). The rigidity of iron interrupts lumpenness (Thesis 9: 'clash: organic form/

mechanical shape') and shifts relative forces (Thesis 31: 'tilt – angle'); it holds spaces open, avoiding collisions as it activates directionality (Thesis 15: 'Two way axial movement'). The rods are movable, managing dynamic interactions as they emerge between lumpen weightings and surfaces. In Jevrić's process cement and plaster have borderline characteristics, having soft and mobile qualities in production that leave traces in the hard substance of the finished works. The metal also had a fluid state which is now solidified. The fact that rust liquefies and penetrates through cement is an important affective factor, perhaps overlooked in sculptural terms. Thesis 12, 'Expression on the basis of analogous exteriorisation of a psychogenic element', holds this sense of exteriorising hidden meaning as expressive entropy incorporated and continuing within the sculptural form.

In spite of the cement's impression of gravity, throughout the work there are varied comparative sensations of weight, as if the more gravity is sensed in one form, the more its counterpart form can levitate, or even circumnavigate through space. This quality connects the sculptures' entropic dynamics to universal forces, from the speed of light to the slow, minutely graduated forces of decay or geological change. Hamlet's view of time being 'out of joint', without measurable sequence or reliable synchronicity, brings heavenly and earthly forces into collision, but in Jevrić's work collision miraculously, or dangerously, fails to happen. There is a filmic, optical watchfulness wherein focal alignments are brought into dynamic capture, moment by moment. This timing of optical activity relates to the motility or mortality of the handling of form. The speeds at which perception seeks transitions of modelling and folding across surfaces becomes codified as differential rates of movement: from glancing into apertures, to sliding across surfaces, to the gaze that attempts to recognise some structuring 'thing'.

Movements of the eye across the work are timed in graduated curvatures, stackings and foldings that originally played, and now continue to play, into the forming and reforming of the work. Jevrić's terminology emphasises plasticity and rhythm. These are standard modernist ideas, but Jevrić reveals them not so much as qualities to be composed but as unities of 'existences and mysteries' or 'harmony in the illusion of dis-harmony'. Jevrić's modelling brings timing to different movements of light to shadow, not in order to differentiate light from dark but to measure transitions dependent on variable curvatures of surface. Thesis 41, 'concave–convex continuities' envisages continuous encounter produced through modulated forms to achieve a 'Unity of complementarity against destructive split'. Into the surfaces of the sculptures are impressed holes, hollows, planes and ridges; these are physical events distinguished through their timing of luminous effect, a soft fade, a darkening recess, an externalised movement of light reflected outward to the viewer rather than an internal glow. Light is used as a medium of continuity rather than for its disruptive possibilities of gleam, scatter or flicker.

Each sculpture offers a consistent reception of ambient light that evolves moment by moment as the viewer circles the sculpture rather than confronts it. This is evident in the film of Jevrić moving continuously around her works, experiencing their changes.[10] Thesis 19 is relevant: 'Sum of actions – poly-psychogenicity'. Jevrić's processual concerns engage with how the work becomes visible through anachronous relations; the timing of the sculpture's assembly; the filmic temporality of perception of revelations and disappearances; the way these coexist in time and out of time with material changes: from powder – liquid - stone, from iron to oxide stain, from insertions of iron structure to dynamic force, from entropic change. The watchfulness of Jevrić's material processing brings a unity in which, as Thesis 18 says: 'Nothing is indifferent – everything is relative'. In Thesis 33 Jevrić compares the instinctive observation of a 'right place' to correctly sensing the pure reverberant quality of 'tuned sound'.

Jevrić was interested in the modernist utilitarian idea that monuments could function to liaise social ideals into everyday experience. In the context of Tito's Yugoslavia, one possible function was to echo a social model related to the renewals of Socialist architecture.[11] An emphasis on unifying and liaison in Jevrić's 'Theses' and 'Unities' may underlie the historic involvement with several projects for public artworks in the ideologically-charged circumstances of postwar Yugoslavia. Some larger-scale versions of works were fabricated, but in the current exhibitions the question of scale is uncertain: maquette or miniature? Perhaps the potential for remaking sculpture in other materials could be seen as participating in a celebrated modernist project, of transmissibility. In this essay the specificity of the materials in which the sculptures have been presented has been taken as constitutive of final meaning, understood as part of the work's emotional entropy: the history of its impermanence on one hand, but a yearning for some other scale and presence on the other.

The aim to work at a larger scale and in bronze conveys Jevrić's longing for the sculptures to attain a more impressive public presence. Perhaps it was always already known that such ambition was unlikely to be realised. The exhibitions at PEER and Handel Street Projects are sympathetic to the works in their current state and sensitive to their fragility – true to the terms of Jevrić's own manifesto as presented in the '43 Theses' and 'Unities'. The works as seen in these exhibitions reflect contemporary doubts about the function and position of such monuments. Perhaps a case in point is Phyllida Barlow's sculpture, which has been considered, in contemporary critical writing, to be anti-monumental and as engaging a

feminist, anti-masculinist strategy. To impute such motives to Jevrić's work would be problematic in historic terms, although such considerations could inform its current reception. For the small scale of works in the exhibition, values remain precious. The works record a consistently caring, thoughtful analysis of touch as discourse. Their forms feel non-specific in origin, emerging from a nucleic core but built up instinctively – sometimes over years – from a continuity of immediate responses towards a 'correlation of nodal points' (Thesis 16). The *povera* material qualities articulate sculptural struggle, but this is appropriate to Jevrić's effort to analyse a vast and abstract range of associations between ideas, material influences and historical events. The fluency with which such disparities are resolved brings memorable grace and poise to Jevrić's works.

NOTES

1 The lists were displayed in the exhibition 'Olga Jevrić: Spatial Compositions' at Handel Street Projects, 28 June–31 October 2019.

2 See Karl Marx, 'Theses on Feuerbach', in *The German Ideology*, part 1 (ed. C.J. Arthur), London 1974, pp.121–23. Thesis V: 'Feuerbach, not satisfied with *abstract* thinking, wants contemplation; but he does not conceive sensuousness as *practical,* human sensuous activity'. That is understood to mean that practical sensuous contact with materials is the source of noumenal ideation. Thesis VIII: 'All social life is essentially *practical*. All mysteries which lead theory to mysticism find their rational solution in human practice and in the comprehension of this practice'. [Marx's italics].

3 I am indebted to a conversation with Lilian Somerville, Director of the Fine Arts Department, British Council, 1947-1970: at the end of an extremely costly war it was important to make an ethical statement about the values that had sustained a conflict in a period of continuing postwar hardship. The biennale movement, with which she was closely involved as organiser and as the selector of works for exhibition, was viewed as a statement that sustained a sense of positive historic purpose.

4 Jevric was aware of contemporary European movements in art. The concept of '*art informel*' was widely interpreted in the postwar period including by the influential movements of Art Brut and CoBrA, and artists such as Dubuffet, Fautrier, Fontana, Burri, Wols, Kemeny, Turnbull, Chadwick.

5 Clement Greenberg, 'Collage', in *Art and Culture: Critical Essays*, Boston 1961, pp.70-83 and 'The Crisis of the Easel Picture' in *The Collected Essays and Criticism*, vol. 2, 1945-49, Chicago 1988, pp.221-25.

6 Jacques Derrida, *Specters of Marx* (trans. Peggy Kamuf), New York and London, 1994, pp.22-25.

7 Derrida, *op. cit.*, p.22.

8 *Olga Jevrić*, filmed discussion between Phyllida Barlow and Richard Deacon of Olga Jevrić's sculpture, presented by Ingrid Swenson, PEER, London, 9 September 2019, https://vimeo.com/359987405.

9 Rosalind Krauss, 'Entropy' in Yve-Alain Bois and Rosalind Krauss, *Formless a Users Guide*, New York 1997, p.77.

10 Olga Jevrić, 'Space and Time', TV Belgrade 1982, production: V. Krčmar, D. Blažević and D. Zupanc: https://vimeo.com/344576753.

11 I am grateful to Fedja Klikovac at Handel Street Projects for providing contextual information.

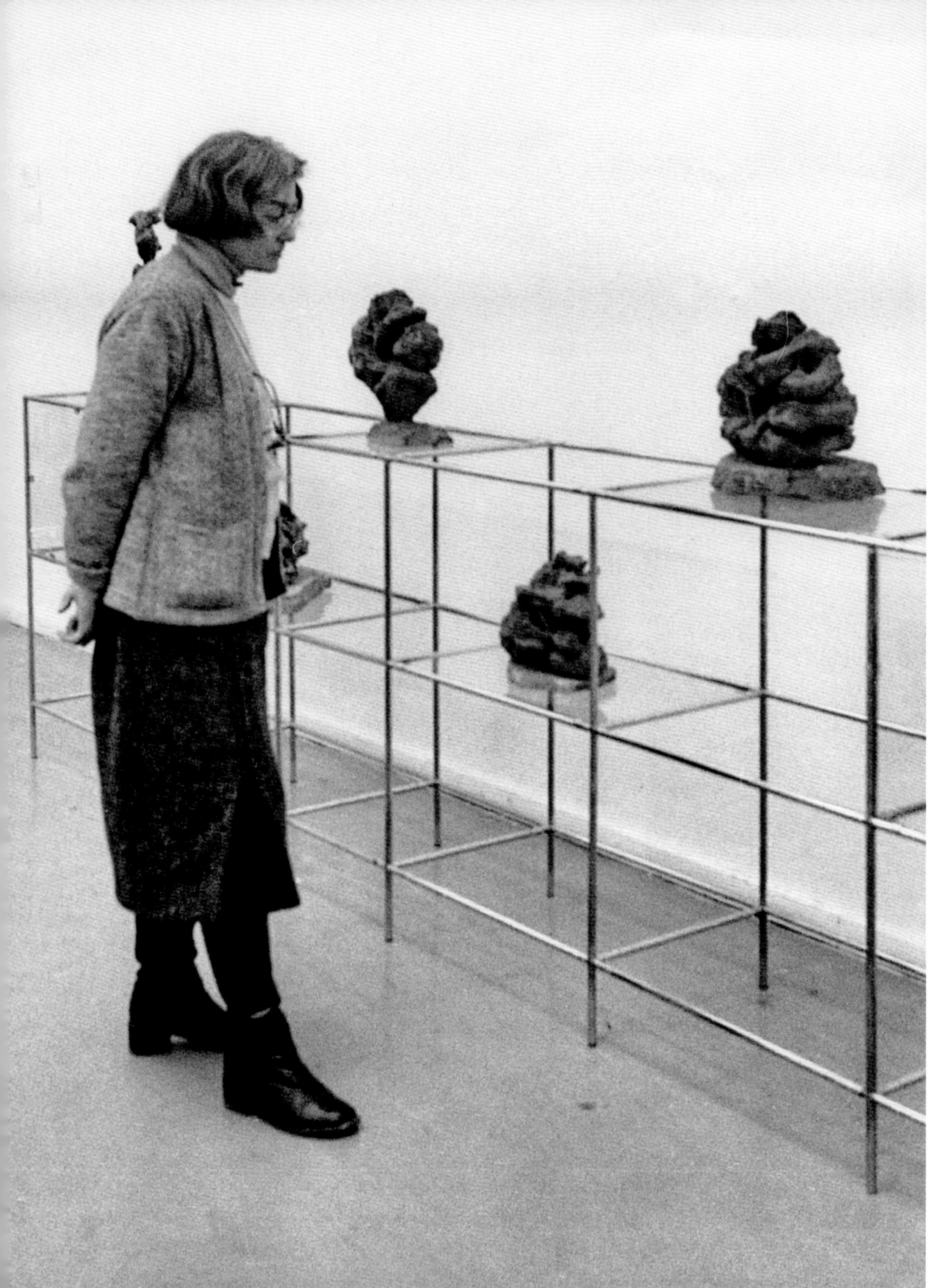

Olga Jevrić at her exhibition at the
Students' Cultural Centre Gallery,
Belgrade, 1988

Photographic credits

© Mrdjan Bajić: p.19

© Digital Archive of the
Heritage House, Belgrade: pp.2, 4,
36–42, cover (front and back)

© FXP Photography: pp.68–77

© Rosa Harvest: pp.27, 33, 34, 86

© Lucy Heyward: pp.8–9, 10, 11, 12, 16

© Museum of Contemporary Art,
Belgrade: pp.22, 81, 82

© Ingrid Swenson: pp.29, 30

© Stephen White: pp.46–67

PEER **Ridinghouse**

Published in 2019 by Ridinghouse in association with PEER

Accompanies the exhibitions
Olga Jevrić: Sculpture
28 June–14 September 2019, PEER
and *Olga Jevrić: Spatial Compositions*
28 June–31 October 2019, Handel Street Projects

Ridinghouse
46 Lexington Street · London W1F 0LP · United Kingdom
ridinghouse.co.uk

PEER
97–99 Hoxton Street , London N1 6QL
peeruk.org

Distributed in the UK and Europe by Cornerhouse Publications
c/o Home · 2 Tony Wilson Place · Manchester M15 4FN
United Kingdom cornerhousepublications.org

Distributed in the United States and Canada by ARTBOOK | D.A.P.
75 Broad Street, Suite 630 · New York, New York 10004
artbook.com

Texts © Phyllida Barlow, Richard Deacon, Ješa Denegri, Joan Key,
Fedja Klikovac and Ingrid Swenson
For the book in this form © Ridinghouse

British Library Cataloguing-in-Publication Data
*A full catalogue record of this book is available from the
British Library.*

ISBN 978 1 909932 57 9

Ridinghouse Publisher: Sophie Kullmann
Designed by Dalrymple
Set in MVB Solitaire
Printed in Verona by Verona Libri

Translation (Ješa Denegri essay): Irena Šentevska

Supported by the Henry Moore Foundation

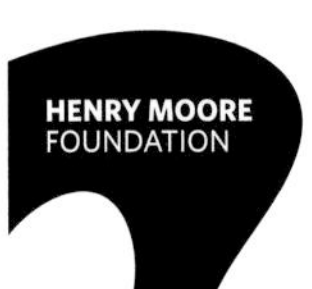